In Search *of* Certitude

DEEPENING OUR UNDERSTANDING STRENGTHENING OUR FAITH

Extracts from the Bahá'í Writings
with introduction and notes by Geoffrey Gore

NINE PINES PUBLISHING
CANADA

Nine Pines Publishing
26 Concourse Gate
Nepean, ON K2E 7T7
Canada

© Geoffrey Gore 1998
All Rights Reserved
G.N. Gore, c/- National Spiritual Assembly of the Bahá'ís of New Zealand, PO Box 21551, Henderson, Auckland, New Zealand

Approved for publication by the National Spiritual Assembly of the Bahá'ís of New Zealand
ISBN 1-895456-16-9

Acknowledgements
Audio-Visual Department of the Universal House of Justice for images of 'Abdu'l-Bahá and Shoghi Effendi

Beverley Rennie for original photographs
Margot Macphail for design and layout

Printed in Canada

Opposite:
Photograph of the Master, 'Abdu'l-Bahá, walking up Haparsim Street, Haifa, Palestine

Meditation from the Writings of 'Abdu'l-Bahá

Briefly, the Blessed Perfection bore all these ordeals and calamities in order that our hearts might become enkindled and radiant, our spirits be glorified, our faults become virtues, our ignorance be transformed into knowledge; in order that we might attain the real fruits of humanity and acquire heavenly graces; in order that, although pilgrims upon earth, we should travel the road of the heavenly Kingdom, and, although needy and poor, we might receive the treasures of eternal life.

Promulgation of Universal Peace, p 28

Introduction

This compilation explores the concept of becoming spiritually strong – a condition referred to in the Bahá'í Holy Writings as 'firmness in the Covenant'. Beginning with the heart and then looking at the importance of vision and understanding, the process of becoming spiritually strong is treated as an exciting journey of discovery, leading to a condition of spiritual happiness and true liberty. To reach that condition is to fulfil the spiritual destiny of the soul, and attain what Bahá'u'lláh describes as *"...the City of Certitude"*. Other vital aspects of the Faith, such as community life, the Administrative Order, and relating to Institutions are dealt with in the light of this journey of the soul, a theme which provides some connection between each section.

By design, a significant proportion of the references used are excerpts from the writings of Shoghi Effendi, the Guardian of the Bahá'í Faith, or from letters written on his behalf. These writings open our eyes to the beauty and power of the Revelation of Bahá'u'lláh, and lend weight to the thought that a lifetime of study would hardly allow sufficient time to absorb the outpouring of divine knowledge contained in this Revelation. It is overwhelming, it is profound, and we need help if we are to understand and appreciate it. This is the Guardian's gift to us all. He helps us to make sense of the spiritual processes going on both within us, and around us. The process within is shown to be a journey of personal discovery and spiritual growth – a preparation for the moment of physical death, when the soul moves into the spiritual worlds of God. At the same time, around us and affecting us, are the powerful and disruptive forces moving humanity towards its promised spiritual and material destiny. The Guardian reveals the origin of these forces, and explains their necessity.

When someone joins the Bahá'í community, the sheer volume of both the Revealed Word and books written about the Faith can be so overwhelming that during the deepening process, certain fundamental principles so necessary to becoming spiritually strong are not understood. As a consequence, some Bahá'ís, even years on, find themselves ill-equipped, in a spiritual sense, to deal with the tests and difficulties which inevitably arise in the course of their lives.

It is therefore an advantage to gain, at the earliest possible time, an overall appreciation of the Covenant of Bahá'u'lláh, and its pivotal importance in the life of the individual, the Bahá'í community and the body of humanity. This brief compilation may help the new Bahá'í to glimpse its greatness, and to catch and hold in the mind a vision of how it is going to transform humanity. Hopefully, it also covers enough aspects of the Faith to help prepare newcomers for Bahá'í community life, and assist them to more rapidly assimilate new information as it is encountered.

Having a vision and an understanding of what lies ahead enables us to put the rest of our lives into proper perspective. Whatever happens from hour to hour or from day to day, one thing remains constant, and that is, that in the Bahá'í Holy Writings can be found the knowledge and the vision which gives total meaning to our existence, and to the events taking place around us.

Those of us who have learnt of this new Faith may never fully appreciate how fortunate we have been. *"Would that we had ten thousand lives,"* 'Abdu'l-Bahá has written, *"that we might lay them down in thanksgiving for so rare a privilege, so high an attainment, so priceless a bounty!"* [*World Order of Bahá'u'lláh*, p110]

There may be times throughout our lives when we feel disconnected from the spiritual reality of Bahá'u'lláh's Faith, and experience it as if through veils, which hide its true power and potency from us. Those who through their own determination lift those veils aside, and enable their souls to experience a fuller measure of Bahá'u'lláh's Revelation find themselves transformed. The rapid growth of this Faith worldwide is a testimony to ordinary people who have experienced such changes in themselves and have gone on to achieve extraordinary and astonishing victories for the Faith they love.

This book is gratefully dedicated to the memory of Shirley Charters, Mary O'Neill and my mother Lilian, whose lives of obedience and service are treasured up for eternity.

Geoffrey Gore
Golden Bay, New Zealand

March 1998

Staircase at Mazra'ih where Bahá'u'lláh lived 1877 - 1879

Meditation from the Writings of Bahá'u'lláh on Knowledge

In like manner, endeavour to comprehend the meaning of the "changing of the earth." Know thou, that upon whatever hearts the bountiful showers of mercy, raining from the "heaven" of divine Revelation, have fallen, the earth of those hearts hath verily been changed into the earth of divine knowledge and wisdom. What myrtles of unity hath the soil of their hearts produced! What blossoms of true knowledge and wisdom hath their illumined bosoms yielded! Were the earth of their hearts to remain unchanged, how could such souls who have not been taught one letter, have seen no teacher, and entered no school, utter such words and display such knowledge as none can apprehend? Methinks they have been moulded from the clay of infinite knowledge, and kneaded with the water of divine wisdom. Therefore, hath it been said: "Knowledge is a light which God casteth into the heart of whomsoever He willeth." It is this kind of knowledge which is and hath ever been praiseworthy, and not the limited knowledge that hath sprung forth from veiled and obscured minds.

Kitáb-í-Iqán, p46

'Abdu'l-Bahá's eldest grandson, Shoghi Effendi, Guardian of the Bahá'í Faith.
"Look at his eyes, they are like clear water," said 'Abdu'l-Bahá.

IN SEARCH OF CERTITUDE

DEEPENING OUR UNDERSTANDING
STRENGTHENING OUR FAITH

EXTRACTS FROM THE BAHA'I WRITINGS
WITH ANNOTATIONS

CONTENTS

Meditations from the Writings 'Abdu'l-Bahá	3
Introduction	4
Meditations from the Writings of Bahá'u'lláh	7
1. The Heart	11
2. Understanding and Vision	22
3. The Covenant	38
4. The Administrative Order	50
5. The Individual and the Community	66
6. Understanding Covenant-Breaking	79
References	98
Bibliography	102
Index of Subtitles	104

In the gardens at Bahjí

1 • THE HEART

It is the desire first born in the human heart which causes the lover to begin searching for the beloved.

Bahá'u'lláh explains that God created us to love:

"Having created the world and all that liveth and moveth therein, He, through the direct operation of His unconstrained and sovereign Will, chose to confer upon man the unique distinction and capacity to know Him and love Him – a capacity that must needs be regarded as the generating impulse and the primary purpose underlying the whole of creation..." [1]

Further, He explained the spiritual significance of the heart in such words as:

"O Son of Being! Thy heart is My home; sanctify it for My descent. Thy spirit is My place of revelation; cleanse it for My manifestation." [2]

"He...hath singled out the hearts of men as His Own domain." [3]

"Out of the whole world He hath chosen for Himself the hearts of men – hearts which the hosts of revelation and of utterance can subdue." [4]

"O friend, the heart is the dwelling of eternal mysteries, make it not the home of fleeting fancies; waste not the treasure of thy precious life in employment with this swiftly passing world. Thou comest from the world of holiness – bind not thine heart to the earth; thou art a dweller in the court of nearness – choose not the homeland of the dust." [5]

Developing Our Spiritual Nature

The purpose in exploring the subject of the heart and the journey of the soul is to show the importance of developing the spirituality hidden within us. The way we live our lives here on earth prepares the soul for its journey through the spiritual worlds of God.

'Abdu'l-Bahá has stated:

> "...We must strive unceasingly and without rest to accomplish the development of the spiritual nature in man, and endeavour with tireless energy to advance humanity toward the nobility of its true and intended station. For the body of man is accidental; it is of no importance. The time of its disintegration will inevitably come. But the spirit of man is essential and therefore eternal. It is a divine bounty. It is the effulgence of the Sun of Reality and therefore of greater importance than the physical body." 6

Bahá'u'lláh warns those who only seek after material things:

> "Say: If ye be seekers after this life and the vanities thereof, ye should have sought them while ye were still enclosed in your mothers' wombs, for at that time ye were continually approaching them, could ye but perceive it. Ye have, on the other hand, ever since ye were born and attained maturity, been all the while receding from the world and drawing closer to dust." 7

He explains that the Prophets and Messengers of God have been sent down for the sole purpose of guiding and educating us so that we may,

> "...at the hour of death, ascend, in the utmost purity and sanctity and with absolute detachment, to the throne of the Most High." 8

Referring to this event (death), 'Abdu'l-Bahá stated:

> "From the moment the soul leaves the body and arrives in the Heavenly World, its evolution is spiritual, and that evolution is: The approaching unto God." 9

How does Bahá'u'lláh describe the mystical connection between God and Man?

> "O Son of Man!
> Veiled in My immemorial being and in the ancient eternity of My essence, I knew My love for thee; therefore I created thee, have engraved on thee Mine image and revealed to thee My beauty." 10

> "O Son of Man!
> I loved thy creation, hence I created thee. Wherefore, do thou love Me, that I may name thy name and fill thy soul with the spirit of life." 11

> "Thou art My lamp and My light is in thee...." 12

"...within thee have I placed the essence of My light..." 13

"I have breathed within thee a breath of My own Spirit, that thou mayest be My lover ...." 14

"Man is My mystery and I am his mystery." 15

"Verily I say, the human soul is, in its essence, one of the signs of God, a mystery among His mysteries. It is one of the mighty signs of the Almighty, the harbinger that proclaimeth the reality of all the worlds of God. Within it lieth concealed that which the world is now utterly incapable of apprehending." 16

The Journey of the Soul

It should be no surprise to us then, that many people, whether consciously or unconsciously, wish to learn about God, spirituality, the true nature of man, the purpose of existence and so on ...

This restlessness, this desire to satisfy an inner need, is part of us. It is how we were created. It is a spiritual blueprint – a condition which we cannot escape! We find confirmation of this in the Hidden Words of Bahá'u'lláh:

*"O Son of Spirit! My claim on thee is great, it cannot be forgotten.
My grace to thee is plenteous, it cannot be veiled.
My love has made in thee its home, it cannot be concealed.
My light is manifest to thee, it cannot be obscured."* 17

And similarly, the Báb wrote:

"All men have proceeded from God and unto Him shall all return." 18

In His Tablet, *The Seven Valleys*, which traces the spiritual journey of the soul towards God, Bahá'u'lláh refers to the first stage of the journey as the Valley of Search. In this Valley, He writes, *"... the seeker ... will behold many a lover, hasting to seek the Beloved, he will witness a world of desiring ones searching after the One Desired."* 19

Bahá'u'lláh goes on to write:

"On this journey the traveler abideth in every land and dwelleth in every region. In every face, he seeketh the beauty of the Friend; in every country he looketh for the Beloved. He joineth every company, and seeketh fellowship with every soul, that haply in some mind he may uncover the

secret of the Friend, or in some face he may behold the beauty of the Loved One." 20

'Abdu'l-Bahá also, spoke about the journey of the soul:
"Briefly, the journey of the soul is necessary. The pathway of life is the road which leads to divine knowledge and attainment. Without training and guidance the soul could never progress beyond the conditions of its lower nature, which is ignorant and defective." 21

The Object of Our Search

Bahá'u'lláh refers to our search and our restlessness in many other passages.

For instance, regarding our finding rest, He writes:
"Wert thou to speed through the immensity of space and traverse the expanse of heaven, yet thou wouldst find no rest save in submission to Our command and humbleness before Our face." 22

And again, regarding our search, He writes:
"...If thou seekest another than Me, yea, if thou searchest the universe for evermore, thy quest will be in vain." 23

Bahá'u'lláh states that it is the duty of every soul to seek God and love God.
"Unless one recognise God and love Him, his cry shall not be heard in this Day. This is the essence of His Faith, did ye but know it." 24

Acquiring the Spirit of Faith
(the end of the search)

The search is fulfilled, and the yearning of the human spirit is satisfied when it attains to the knowledge of God, recognizes His Messenger, and acquires the spirit of faith.

'Abdu'l-Bahá reveals how important this is when He states:
"But the human spirit, unless assisted by the spirit of faith, does not become acquainted with the divine secrets and the heavenly realities." 25

Christ spoke of it as the 'second birth', and 'Abdu'l-Bahá used the same words to describe it. What is this spirit of faith? 'Abdu'l-Bahá explains:

> "The fourth degree of spirit is the heavenly spirit; it is the spirit of faith and the bounty of God; it comes from the breath of the Holy Spirit, and by the divine power it becomes the cause of eternal life. It is the power which makes the earthly man heavenly, and the imperfect man perfect. It makes the impure to be pure, the silent eloquent; it purifies and sanctifies those made captive by carnal desires; it makes the ignorant wise." 26

He also described it in this way:

> "...You were asleep; you are awakened. Your ears are attentive; your hearts are informed. You have acquired the love of God. You have attained to the knowledge of God. This is the most great bestowal of God. This is the breath of the Holy Spirit, and this consists of faith and assurance. This eternal life is the second birth; this is the baptism of the Holy Spirit. God has destined this station for you all. He has prepared this for you. You must appreciate the value of this bounty and engage your time in mentioning and thanking the True One. You must live in the utmost happiness. If any trouble or vicissitude should come into your lives, if your heart is depressed on account of health, livelihood or vocation, let not these things affect you. They should not cause unhappiness, for Bahá'u'lláh has brought you divine happiness. He has prepared heavenly food for you; He has destined eternal bounty for you; He has bestowed everlasting glory upon you. Therefore, these glad tidings should cause you to soar in the atmosphere of joy forever and ever..." 27

In *The Book of Certitude*, Bahá'u'lláh states that "the spirit of faith" will be

> "...breathed into thy being, and thou shalt be established and abide upon the seat of certitude" when (you) "apprehend the greatness of this Revelation, and perceive its stupendous glory." 28

Becoming Stronger in Your Faith

Faith is relative. Some people have a little, whereas others have a great deal.

Whatever our portion, we must continue to grow ever stronger in our faith. Bahá'í scholar Mr. Adib Taherzadeh explains:

"And if a person's faith does not increase with the passage of time it is like a child which is born but fails to grow. Such a person is very likely to feel a measure of doubt in his innermost heart concerning the Faith, and may experience great conflicts in his mind, especially when he goes through tests. Although intellectually he may accept Bahá'u'lláh as a Manifestation of God and may even be well versed in His Writings, he will not be able to have that absolute certitude which endows a human being with spiritual qualities and confers upon him perpetual contentment, assurance and happiness." 29

The spark of faith needs to be fanned into a flame, and then into a fire. If we wish to burn brightly with our faith, we can – it is our choice. If we make the effort to read and study the Holy Writings, and try sincerely to live our lives according to the principles revealed by Bahá'u'lláh, this spiritual process will lead the believer to love Bahá'u'lláh and to love God.

How Does Somebody "Love God?"

What does that mean?

How does one love God when Bahá'u'lláh Himself tells us that God is the unknowable essence? Similarly, how does one love the Manifestation of God?

Attributes such as love, firmness, steadfastness and faith, are spiritual qualities which are called forth from the soul. When the heart comes into contact with the Revelation of Bahá'u'lláh and becomes convinced of its truth, then the spirit of faith is conceived in that heart. If that person then chooses to act according to the laws and principles revealed by Him, then the soul will be gradually transformed. It will continue to grow and develop, acquiring spiritual qualities, and experience what it is to love God and love His Manifestation.

In a practical sense, this means that we must:
- Pray and meditate
- Recite the obligatory prayers daily
- Read the Writings in the morning and in the evening
- Strive to live our lives according to the teachings
- Share this knowledge with others – teach the faith

If you persevere in this, then you will come to know what it means to love God, to love Bahá'u'lláh. You may not be able to describe that feeling or that condition to someone else, but having experienced it, you will know it to be a reality.

The Importance of Recognising the Manifestation of God

> "The first duty prescribed by God for His servants is the recognition of Him Who is the Dayspring of His Revelation and the Fountain of His laws, Who representeth the Godhead in both the Kingdom of His Cause and the world of creation. Whoso achieveth this duty hath attained unto all good; and whoso is deprived thereof hath gone astray, though he be the author of every righteous deed. It behoveth every one who reacheth this most sublime station, this summit of transcendent glory, to observe every ordinance of Him Who is the Desire of the world. These twin duties are inseparable. Neither is acceptable without the other. Thus hath it been decreed by Him Who is the source of Divine inspiration." 30

Good Deeds Alone Are Not Enough

One of 'Abdu'l-Bahá's comments on the above tablet of Bahá'u'lláh states:

> "Therefore the blessed verse means that the good actions alone, without the knowledge of God, cannot be the cause of eternal salvation, everlasting success, and prosperity, and entrance into the Kingdom of God." 31

Bahá'u'lláh cites **two obligations** for the one who has recognised Him:

Firstly *"... steadfastness in His love"*

Secondly *"... strict observance of the laws He hath prescribed."* 32

And in a similar vein He writes:

> "... Having reached this lofty station a twofold obligation resteth upon every soul. One is to be steadfast in the Cause with such steadfastness that were all the peoples of the world to attempt to prevent him from turning to the Source of Revelation, they would be powerless to do so. The other is observance of the divine ordinances which have streamed forth from the wellspring of His heavenly-propelled pen." 33

Testing Our Faith – the Beginning of Growth

Most people would no doubt prefer to avoid difficulties in their lives, yet according to the Bahá'í Writings, tests and difficulties are inevitable, and are to be welcomed, since overcoming them stimulates our spiritual growth.

Indeed, Bahá'u'lláh states that some tests are sent by God to prove our sincerity, and He confirms how inescapable this process is, by referring so frequently throughout His Writings to the need for steadfastness.

> *"Meditate profoundly, that the secret of things unseen may be revealed unto you, that you may inhale the sweetness of a spiritual and imperishable fragrance, and that you may acknowledge the truth that from time immemorial even unto eternity the Almighty hath tried, and will continue to try, His servants, so that light may be distinguished from darkness, truth from falsehood, right from wrong, guidance from error, happiness from misery, and roses from thorns. Even as He hath revealed: "Do men think when they say 'We believe' they shall be let alone and not be put to proof?"* 34

'Abdu'l-Bahá said that steadfastness is necessary to: *"...withstand the hidden and evident tests."* 35

And in a letter written on his behalf, the Guardian of the Bahá'í Faith, Shoghi Effendi, stressed the need for the believers to be:

> *"...truly firm, deep, spiritually convinced Bahá'ís."* 36

He further stated that:

> *"Firmness in the Covenant is their Fortress, their greatest protection, and new Bahá'ís should be taught this before they are admitted into the Community. In this way they will be given the spiritual strength to overcome the tests which are inevitable, and which strengthen the growth of the Community and drive its roots deeper in the soil of faith."* 37

 ## The Heart Must Love God

It seems then that our firmness or steadfastness as Bahá'ís will depend not on our 'intellectual grasp of the teachings', but on something far more profound – love.

It is the nature of the heart to love. If it does not love God, it will become attracted to love of self, and the things of this world.

Bahá'u'lláh warns us of this repeatedly:

> "Wouldst thou have Me, seek none other than Me; and wouldst thou gaze on My beauty, close thine eyes to the world and all that is therein; for My will and the will of another than Me, even as fire and water, cannot dwell together in one heart." 38

> "Set not your affections on things below." 39

> "...Set not your affections on mortal sovereignty and rejoice not therein." 40

> "Ye have suffered My enemy to enter My house and have cast out My friend, for ye have enshrined the love of another than Me in your hearts." 41

And then, throughout the Hidden Words in the most moving and beautiful language, He pleads with us to turn our loving capacity, our hearts towards Him, towards God. He even relates our creation to love!

> "...Out of the clay of love I moulded thee, how dost thou busy thyself with another...?" 42

> "...My love is in thee, know it, that thou mayest find Me near unto thee." 43

> "Love Me, that I may love thee. If thou lovest Me not, My love can in no wise reach thee. Know this, O servant." 44

> "In the garden of thy heart plant naught but the rose of love...." 45

> "...Make My love thy treasure and cherish it even as thy very sight and life." 46

> "I belong to him that loveth Me, that holdeth fast My commandments, and casteth away the things forbidden him in My Book." 47

> "Earth and heaven cannot contain Me; what can alone contain me is the heart of him that believeth in Me, and is faithful to My Cause" 48

 ## Love Transforms, and Love Changes Our Reality

It is through love that we will find the fulfilment of our spiritual search.

In the *Kitáb-í-Iqán*, Bahá'u'lláh describes how the love in a seeker's heart will lead eventually to the soul's experiencing life in a completely new way:

> "*Only when the lamp of search, of earnest striving, of longing desire, of passionate devotion, of fervid love, of rapture, and ecstasy, is kindled within the seeker's heart, and the breeze of His loving-kindness is wafted upon his soul, will the darkness of error be dispelled, the mists of doubts and misgivings be dissipated, and the lights of knowledge and certitude envelop his being. At that hour will the mystic Herald, bearing the joyful tidings of the Spirit, shine forth from the City of God resplendent as the morn, and, through the trumpet-blast of knowledge, will awaken the heart, the soul, and the spirit from the slumber of negligence. Then will the manifold favours and outpouring grace of the holy and everlasting Spirit confer such new life upon the seeker that he will find himself endowed with a new eye, a new ear, a new heart, and a new mind. He will contemplate the manifest signs of the universe, and will penetrate the hidden mysteries of the soul. Gazing with the eye of God, he will perceive within every atom a door that leadeth him to the stations of absolute certitude. He will discover in all things the mysteries of divine Revelation and the evidences of an everlasting manifestation.*" 49

1 • THE HEART

SUMMARY

There is a mystical connection between God and man. In creating us, God breathed into us a breath of His own spirit, and engraved our hearts with His own image in order that we could know Him and love Him.

It is most important that we develop spirituality, because the death of our physical body is inevitable, whereas the spirit of man is eternal, and is destined to progress through the spiritual worlds of God.

The soul seeks God because it was created by God and yearns to return to Him.

When the soul gains knowledge of God and recognizes His Messenger, **it acquires the spirit of faith**, it finds rest and its yearning is satisfied.

Acquiring the spirit of faith is, by itself, not enough. This signals the end of the search, but it also initiates a new phase of spiritual growth. After recognition, **steadfastness and obedience are necessary** to enable the soul to overcome the tests associated with its spiritual journey.

As we strive to act according to the laws and principles revealed by God's Messenger, our **souls will gradually be transformed** and we will know what it means to love God and to love Baha'u'llah. How firm and steadfast we remain in God's Faith will depend upon how much our hearts become attached to God and to the teachings of His Messenger.

As the lights of knowledge and certitude envelop the soul, God confers a new life upon it. It will seem to the seeker that he or she is endowed with a new eye, a new ear, a new heart, and a new mind.

21

2 • UNDERSTANDING AND VISION

Regarding the favours bestowed by God on mankind, Bahá'u'lláh states:

> *"First and foremost ... is the gift of understanding. ... Next in rank, is the power of vision, the chief instrument whereby his understanding can function."* [1]

Having turned our hearts to God, and acquired the spirit of faith, understanding and vision is needed to sustain and guide us throughout our lives. Without understanding and vision, it is difficult to achieve goals. With understanding and vision we are more likely to act, to do something.

Vision can provide the most powerful motivation for the service we give to the Faith, our work, our family, our fellow Bahá'ís and to those we meet in the course of our lives. Bahá'u'lláh placed great emphasis on it:

> *"...This vision acteth as the agent and guide for true knowledge."* [2]

The City of Certitude

We increase our understanding and develop our vision by reading and studying the Holy Writings. Of particular importance is study of the *Kitáb-i-Iqán – The Book of Certitude*. In it, Bahá'u'lláh describes in a marvellous way the spiritual bounties awaiting the seeker who will "attain and enter the City of Certitude."

He goes on to say:

> *"The attainment of this City quencheth thirst without water, and kindleth the love of God without fire.... It bestoweth wealth without gold, and conferreth immortality without death. In every leaf ineffable delights are treasured, and within every chamber unnumbered mysteries lie hidden."* [3]

What Is This City?

The City of Certitude is the revealed Word of God: today, the Writings of Bahá'u'lláh, and especially, the Most Holy Book, the *Kitáb-í-Aqdás*.

This City (the Writings) contains spiritual sustenance, knowledge, guidance, blessings, learning, understanding, faith and certitude.

> "That city is none other than the Word of God revealed in every age and dispensation. In the days of Moses it was the Pentateuch; in the days of Jesus the Gospel; in the days of Muhammad the Messenger of God the Qur'an; in this day the Bayan; and in the dispensation of Him Whom God will make manifest* His own Book – the Book unto which all the Books of former Dispensations must needs be referred, the Book which standeth amongst them all transcendent and supreme. In these cities spiritual sustenance is bountifully provided, and incorruptible delights have been ordained. The food they bestow is the bread of heaven, and the spirit they impart is God's imperishable blessing. Upon detached souls they bestow the gift of Unity, enrich the destitute, and offer the cup of knowledge unto them who wander in the wilderness of ignorance. All the guidance, the blessings, the learning, the understanding, the faith, and certitude, conferred upon all that is in heaven and on earth, are hidden and treasured within these Cities." 4

[* Bahá'u'lláh wrote this some time before His declaration]

When we begin to appreciate the wealth of knowledge contained within His Writings, we will want to immerse ourselves in them, and will feel bereft without them. In His *Kitáb-í-Aqdás* Bahá'u'lláh Himself stressed the importance of reading the revealed Word of God:

> "Recite ye the verses of God every morn and eventide. Whoso faileth to recite them hath not been faithful to the Covenant of God and His Testament, and whoso turneth away from these holy verses in this Day is of those who throughout eternity have turned away from God." 5

He goes on to say that we should do this with **joy** and **gladness,** that this action will cause our hearts to be suffused with light, cause our souls to soar, and bring us nearer to God.

The Writings – Reading to Understand

The Revelation of Bahá'u'lláh covers a vast range of writings which include prayers, prophecies, spiritual teachings, proclamations to kings, rulers, religious leaders and peoples of the world, as well as laws and ordinances.

Shoghi Effendi, the Guardian of the Faith, likened Bahá'u'lláh's Revelation to a sun whose *"rays were to burst forth"* over the entire world, radiating *"a power, a radiance and a glory"* (6) which would resurrect mankind.

The purpose in reading these writings, Bahá'u'lláh says, should be to understand the meanings and unravel the mysteries.

> *"Otherwise reading, without understanding, is of no abiding profit unto man."* 7

- Vision affects understanding.
- Vision helps us to understand what we read, hear, see and experience.
- Vision keeps us focused on our goals.
- Vision can influence: * Our achievements

    * Our spiritual development and happiness

    * Our family and our community

    * The evolution of the entire human family

In the various areas of human endeavour, there have always been individuals who have shown the way forward through their vision, exceptional knowledge and ability. In the field of religious endeavour, which today sees the Bahá'ís involved in the spiritual conquest of the planet, the beloved Guardian, Shoghi Effendi, assumed this key role of providing leadership and vision. Apart from the three central figures of the Faith, namely the Báb, Bahá'u'lláh and 'Abdu'l-Bahá, he was perhaps the only person to fully appreciate the greatness of Bahá'u'lláh's Revelation, to see it as a whole, to understand its importance and to share his insights with us.

Shoghi Effendi – the Importance of Reading His Writings

The Guardianship is an Institution of the Faith.

In a most significant letter entitled *The Dispensation of Bahá'u'lláh*, Shoghi Effendi wrote that *"Without such an institution ... [as the Guardianship] ... the means required to enable it [the Faith] to take a long, an uninterrupted view over a series of generations would be completely lacking ..."* 8

Providing us with a vision of the future is perhaps one of the most important aspects of the Guardian's ministry. The more we read his writings, the more we will appreciate how fortunate we are to have this perspective. In his role as interpreter of Bahá'u'lláh's Writings, he broadened our vision and pointed the way forward. Rúhíyyih Khánum once wrote of him: "He had not only the capacity to see but to analyze and express with brilliant clarity what he saw." 9

Understanding the Revelation of Bahá'u'lláh

When we as individuals try to understand the purpose of His Revelation and what is asked of us as His followers, we have difficulty taking it all in.

He (Bahá'u'lláh) Himself used such words as **bewildering, resplendent, pervasive, most mighty, stupendously glorious, wondrous,** when describing His Own Revelation. In fact, He states that the reason this Revelation is given to us in words, is due to our weakness and frailty.

"... otherwise," He declares, *" the Cause We have proclaimed is such as no pen can ever describe, nor any mind conceive its greatness."* 10

This is why the function of the Guardian is so important in the Faith. Shoghi Effendi has illuminated, interpreted and explained the Writings of Bahá'u'lláh for us. If we study his writings, our understanding will increase, and we will develop a vision of God's purpose for humanity.

He pointed out that Bahá'u'lláh's message applied to the whole world, not just to individuals. He explained that the goal of the Faith was to re-create society, to create a world civilization which would in turn, have a wonderful effect upon the individuals within it. These two processes must, he said, go hand in hand – the transformation of society and the transformation of personal character.

Taking the Administrative Order into Our Vision

It is absolutely vital that we include the Administrative Order in our vision of the Faith. It is the tool, the vehicle, the means by which the spirit of Bahá'u'lláh will transform this world and create a new, spiritual civilization.

Shoghi Effendi, throughout his own writings, constantly quoted from the Writings of Bahá'u'lláh. He underlined the importance of the Administrative Order and explained the principle that religion by itself was not enough to heal the world. He said:

> "...the Spirit breathed by Bahá'u'lláh upon the world ... can never permeate" and have a lasting effect on humanity "unless and until it incarnates itself in a visible Order ..." [11]

He then set about building the Administrative Order on the foundations laid by Bahá'u'lláh and 'Abdu'l-Bahá. Throughout his 36-year ministry, he nurtured it, and educated and trained the Bahá'ís to ensure that this divine system of government was very firmly established throughout the world.

A Pattern for Future Society

Shoghi Effendi helped us to appreciate the importance of the Administrative Order by telling us that the laws and principles upon which its Institutions were based are: "...*destined to be a pattern for future society, a supreme instrument for the establishment of the Most Great Peace, and the one agency for the unification of the world ...*"[12]

He further stated:

> "It implies an organic change in the structure of present-day society, a change such as the world has not yet experienced."

> "It represents the consummation of human evolution ..." [13]

> "The emergence of a world community, the consciousness of world citizenship, the founding of a world civilisation and culture – all of which

must synchronize with the initial stages in the unfoldment of the Golden Age of the Bahá'í Era – should, by their very nature, be regarded, as far as this planetary life is concerned, as the furthermost limits in the organization of human society ..." 14

And to those who would say Bahá'ís are just wishful thinkers, he leaves no doubt as to the power within the Administrative Order in this resounding statement:

"Let there be no mistake. The principle of the Oneness of Mankind – the pivot round which all the teachings of Bahá'u'lláh revolve – is no mere outburst of ignorant emotionalism or an expression of vague and pious hope. ... It does not constitute merely the enunciation of an ideal, but stands inseparably associated with an institution adequate to embody its truth, demonstrate its validity, and perpetuate its influence." 15

Vision of the Future – Looking Ahead to the Goal

From time to time, Shoghi Effendi lifted our eyes to a distant horizon and stirred our imaginations by describing what society will be like in the future.

These words are taken from one of his letters to the Bahá'ís of the West in 1936:

"A world metropolis will act as the nerve centre of a world civilisation, the focus towards which the unifying forces of life will converge and from which its energizing influences will radiate ...

National rivalries, hatreds, and intrigues will cease, and racial animosity and prejudice will be replaced by racial amity, understanding and cooperation ... The enormous energy dissipated and wasted on war ... will be consecrated to such ends as will extend the range of human inventions and technical development ... to the extermination of disease, to the extension of scientific research, to the raising of the standard of physical health, to the sharpening and refinement of the human brain, to the exploitation of the unused and unsuspected resources of the planet, to the prolongation of human life..." 16

Having given us this vision, he then set about to explain the stages and processes which the faith and humanity will go through in order to reach the goal.

Stages in the Development of the Faith of Bahá'u'lláh

Shoghi Effendi explained that the Faith would go through a number of stages, before reaching the ultimate goal of world civilization.

These stages he listed as:

Obscurity – being unknown and not understood
Repression – being put down by force
Emancipation – being set free
Recognition – being recognised for what it really is
Establishment – the stage at which the Faith of Bahá'u'lláh will be recognised by civil authorities as the state religion.
Emergence of the Bahá'í State itself, which will eventually culminate in the establishment of the World Bahá'í Commonwealth (leading to the Kingdom of God on earth as promised by Christ).
This final stage (the World Bahá'í Commonwealth) *"...will, in turn, prove to be the signal for the **birth of a World Civilization**, incomparable in its range, its character and potency, in the history of mankind ..."* 17

Where are we now in relation to the above stages described by the Guardian?
In their Ridván message of 1986 to the Bahá'ís of the world, the Universal House of Justice announced that the Faith was emerging from obscurity. In the Ridván message the following year, the Universal House of Justice advised that the Administrative Institutions of the Faith were now emerging from obscurity. Since then, each year, the Universal House of Justice has called our attention to the importance of the Bahá'í community being a model, and reflecting a pattern of life that "will rekindle hope among the increasingly disillusioned members of society."

Two Divine Processes

Having outlined the stages ahead, Shoghi Effendi advised us that two divine processes would influence humanity's approach to unity, and *"... bring to a climax the forces that are transforming the face of our planet."* 18

2 • UNDERSTANDING AND VISION

The Seat of the Universal House of Justice in Haifa

He called these the Great Plan of God and the Minor Plan of God.

The Great Plan is breaking down old systems, to bring political unity to the world. This political unity is described as the Lesser Peace.

The Minor Plan of God has to do with the Bahá'ís. It is a building up of a new system which will be a pattern for a new society. The influence of the Minor Plan of God will in time produce a world commonwealth operating according to spiritual principles. This is the Most Great Peace.

The Great Plan of God came about because the kings and rulers rejected the call of Bahá'u'lláh.

> *"The destructive forces that characterize the other should be identified with a civilization that has refused to answer to the expectation of a new age, and is consequently falling into chaos and decline."* [19]
>
> It is *"...fundamentally disruptive."* [19]
>
> It is *"...working through mankind as a whole, tearing down barriers to world unity and forging humankind into a unified body in the fires of suffering and experience."* [20]
>
> Is a *"tempest ...sweeping the face of the earth"* [21]
>
> Is like *"...a great and mighty wind of God invading the remotest and fairest regions of the earth."* [21]
>
> *"This judgement of God ...is both a retributory calamity and an act of holy and supreme discipline. It is ... a visitation from God and a cleansing process for all mankind."* [22]
>
> *"This process will produce, in God's due time, the Lesser Peace, the political unification of the world. Mankind at that time can be likened to a body that is unified but without life."* [23]

The Minor Plan of God is what the Bahá'í community is now carrying out:

> *"The second process, the task of breathing life into this unified body – of creating true unity and spirituality culminating in the Most Great Peace – is that of the Bahá'ís ..."* [23]
>
> It *"...is essentially an integrating process ..."* [24]

Plans – Realising the Vision, Step by Step

The Guardian did not just leave us with a dream-vision of a future ideal world, he made plans for the Bahá'ís to achieve that goal step by step.

Through these teaching plans, he directed the Bahá'ís of the world to focus on the immediate work to be done, the first victories to be won. This is how he made the ultimate goals of Bahá'u'lláh's Revelation attainable, by teaching us to achieve them step by step. As we work to win the goals of each plan, we become stronger, more steadfast Bahá'ís, and our vision becomes reality. Referring to this aspect of the Guardian's leadership, Rúhíyyih Rabbání wrote: "Knowing how prone human nature is to be diverted from any purpose, he constantly reiterated the tasks undertaken, the responsibility assumed, the immediate need." 25

A Great Spiritual Battle

Referring to these two great processes described above, Shoghi Effendi wrote: *"A titanic, a spiritual struggle, unparalleled in its magnitude yet unspeakably glorious in its ultimate consequences, is being waged as a result of these opposing tendencies, in this age of transition ..."* 26

Again, in a cablegram to all National Spiritual Assemblies just months before he died, Shoghi Effendi made a further reference to this spiritual battle:

"Evidences of increasing hostility without, persistent machinations within, foreshadowing dire contests destined to range the Army of Light against the forces of darkness, both secular and religious, predicted ... by 'Abdu'l-Bahá ..." 27

And although his writings clearly depict a great global spiritual struggle, yet still, he drew our attention to how this process challenged us as individuals:

"If we could perceive the true reality of things we would see that the greatest of all battles raging in the world today is the spiritual battle. If the believers like yourself, young and eager and full of life, desire to win laurels for true and undying heroism, then let them join in the spiritual battle – whatever their physical occupation may be – which involves the very soul of man. The hardest and the noblest task in the world today is to be a true Bahá'í; this requires that we defeat not only the current evils prevailing all over the world, but the weaknesses, attachments to the past, prejudices, and selfishnesses that may be inherited and acquired within our own characters; that we give forth a shining and incorruptible example to our fellow-men." 28

The Suffering of Humanity

In many of his letters, the Guardian indicated that humanity will have to undergo a great transformation of *"unparalleled majesty and scope"* [29] to prepare it for the New World Order visualized by Bahá'u'lláh.

He also warned that in order to achieve this transformation, humanity may have to suffer:

> *"That the forces of a world catastrophe can alone precipitate such a new phase of human thought is, alas, becoming increasingly apparent. That nothing short of the fire of a severe ordeal, unparalleled in its intensity, can fuse and weld the discordant entities that constitute the elements of present-day civilization, into the integral components of the world commonwealth of the future, is a truth which future events will increasingly demonstrate."* 29

In another letter written on his behalf in 1946, the Guardian has further stated:

> *"All we know is that the Lesser and the Most Great Peace will come – their exact dates we do not know. The same is true as regards the possibility of a future war; we cannot state dogmatically it will or will not take place – all we know is that mankind must suffer and be punished sufficiently to make it turn to God."* 30

[Note: In the preface to *The World Order of Bahá'u'lláh*, Bahá'í scholar Horace Holley made an interesting observation about the suffering of mankind:

> "When the Word of God is denied, resisted and effort made to destroy its potency, man places himself in opposition to God. From that opposition flow the wars and revolutions which become the instruments by which a non-believing generation inflicts dire punishment upon itself." 31]

A Vision That Prepares Us to Withstand Hidden Tests

As we read earlier, 'Abdu'l-Bahá emphasised the importance of developing our spiritual nature and affirmed that *"...the spirit of man is essential and, therefore, eternal. It is a divine bounty. It is the effulgence of the Sun of Reality and, therefore, of greater importance than the physical body."* 32

Therefore, as Bahá'ís, we must regard the things which take us away from, or prevent us developing, our spiritual natures as our greatest enemies, and the greatest threat to our happiness and well-being. These are the mental tests spoken of by 'Abdu'l-Bahá. Most of us face these tests every day. We live in a society where the majority of people have replaced belief in God with belief in science, and where the development of spiritual certitude has been replaced by the desire to achieve happiness through material wealth and economic security. In a letter written on behalf of Shoghi Effendi in 1935, we read:

> "The universal crisis affecting mankind is, therefore, essentially spiritual in its causes." 33

and in an earlier letter written on his behalf in 1931, we read:

> "Unless society learns to attribute more importance to spiritual matters, it would never be fit to enter the golden era foretold by Bahá'u'lláh. The present calamities are part of this process of purgation, through them alone will man learn his lesson. They are to teach the nations, that they have to view things internationally, they are to make the individual attribute more importance to his moral, than his material welfare." 34

Materialism – a Universal Threat

These are just some of the words used by the Guardian to describe materialism:

'Rampant' (meaning unchecked, unrestrained, aggressive)

'Brutal' (meaning inhuman, savage)

'Excessive' (something going beyond moderation)

'Binding' (the condition of being made captive)

'Enervating' (to weaken mentally or morally; to destroy the capacity for action)

'All-pervasive' (the power to spread throughout)

'Pernicious' (having the quality of destroying, destructive, ruinous, fatal)

'Crass' (coarse, gross, unrefined)

'Cancerous' (the nature of a malignant growth, that tends to spread and reproduce itself. It corrodes the part concerned and generally ends in death.)

[Definitions from Shorter Oxford Dictionary]

In the following quotation, Shoghi Effendi describes how materialism affects people. He then asserts that we Bahá'ís must overcome the mental tests that are associated with it and by doing this, give an example to the world.

> *"The gross materialism that engulfs the entire nation at the present hour; the attachment to worldly things that enshrouds the souls of men; the fear and anxieties that distract their minds; the pleasure and dissipations that fill their time, the prejudices and animosities that darken their outlook, the apathy and lethargy that paralyze their spiritual faculties – these are among the formidable obstacles that stand in the path of every would-be warrior in the service of Bahá'u'lláh, obstacles which he must battle against and surmount in his crusade for the redemption of his own countrymen."* 35

Not only can materialism affect our spiritual faculties, but it also is the cause of enormous suffering to peoples all over the world. The Guardian used the strongest language to denounce it throughout his writings:

> *"It is this same cancerous materialism, born originally in Europe, carried to excess in the North American continent, contaminating the Asiatic peoples and nations, spreading its ominous tentacles to the borders of Africa, and now invading its very heart, which Bahá'u'lláh in unequivocal and emphatic language denounced in His Writings, comparing it to a devouring flame and regarding it as the chief factor in precipitating the dire ordeals and world-shaking crises that must necessarily involve the burning of cities and the spread of terror and consternation in the hearts of men."* 36

The onset of this cancerous materialism is linked to society discarding religion, turning away from God and rejecting His Messenger.

When the Lamp of Religion Is Obscured

Bahá'u'lláh affirmed that *"Religion is the greatest of all means for the establishment of order in the world"* [37] and warned *"Should the lamp of religion be obscured, chaos and confusion will ensue ..."* [38] This is precisely what is happening.

The Guardian described the situation very strongly in the following passage:

> "A world spiritually destitute, morally bankrupt, politically disrupted, socially convulsed, economically paralyzed, writhing, bleeding and breaking up beneath the avenging rod of God. A Faith Whose call remained unanswered, Whose claims were rejected, Whose warnings were brushed aside, Whose followers were mowed down, Whose aims and purposes were maligned, Whose summons to the rulers of the earth were ignored ..." [39]

Effects on Character

Shoghi Effendi gave some examples of what happens to human character " ...*when, as a result of human perversity, the light of religion is quenched in men's hearts ...*"

> "The perversion of human nature, the degradation of human conduct, the corruption and dissolution of human institutions ..."

> "Human character is debased, confidence is shaken, the nerves of discipline are relaxed, the voice of human conscience is stilled, the sense of decency and shame is obscured, conceptions of duty, of solidarity, of reciprocity and loyalty are distorted, and the very feeling of peacefulness, of joy and of hope is gradually extinguished." [40]

Bahá'u'lláh, saddened by the condition of humanity in His Own time, wrote:

> "How long will humanity persist in its waywardness? How long will injustice continue? How long is chaos and confusion to reign amongst men? How long will discord agitate the face of society? ... The winds of despair are, alas, blowing from every direction, and the strife that divideth and afflicteth the human race is daily increasing." [41]

The great challenge facing us as Bahá'ís is to show humanity, **by example**, that this time, the religion of God will bring a day that will not be followed by night. This is why we need to have **vision** and **why we need to study the writings of Shoghi Effendi.**

Arcade of the Shrine of the Báb

2 • UNDERSTANDING AND VISION

SUMMARY

Vision is the guide for true knowledge. Vision has a powerful influence on all aspects of our lives.

It is through **reading the Writings regularly** that we will increase our vision and deepen our understanding.

It is important to **study the writings of Shoghi Effendi.** He alone could see Bahá'u'lláh's design, and enabled us to appreciate the greatness of His Revelation. His vision extended far into the future. Reading Shoghi Effendi's writings will help us visualize our goals more clearly.

Our vision of the Faith must **include the Administrative Order.** It is the channel for the spirit, the vehicle which will carry humanity to the goal of a World Commonwealth operating according to the spiritual principles revealed by Bahá'u'lláh. It will change the structure of present day society.

Understanding the stages the Faith will go through gives depth to our vision. **Knowing where we are now** gives us perspective.

There are **two great processes going on in the world.** One of them is essentially destructive, and began when the world, particularly the kings and rulers of the world, rejected the call of Bahá'u'lláh. It is a punishment, and a cleansing process that will result in a political unity called the Lesser Peace. The other process involves the Bahá'ís and has to do with building up a new system which will be a pattern for a new society. It is a spiritualising process which will eventually produce the Most Great Peace.

Supporting the teaching plans of the Faith is how we show our understanding of the importance of the goals, and turns our vision into reality step by step.

Understand that there is a great spiritual battle going on in the world, and that if we are not steadfast, if we do not remain focused on our goals, then we will be unable to demonstrate the Bahá'í way of life and provide the example that this suffering world so desperately needs.

37

3 • THE COVENANT
AND ITS PLACE IN OUR LIVES

The Covenant is a great power which embraces everything and affects everything.

'Abdu'l-Bahá underlines its importance in the following excerpts:

> *"Today, the Lord of Hosts is the defender of the Covenant, the forces of the Kingdom protect it, heavenly souls tender their services, and heavenly angels promulgate and spread it broadcast. If it is considered with insight, it will be seen that all the forces of the universe, in the last analysis serve the Covenant.* 1

> *"Today the dynamic power of the world of existence is the power of the Covenant which like unto an artery pulsateth in the body of the contingent world ..."* 2

The Covenant is such a vast subject that one needs to read and study the Writings regularly, to gain a better understanding of it. As an introduction, we shall look briefly at three aspects of the Covenant:

1. The Covenant and the Heart
2. The Covenant and the Messengers of God
3. The Covenant and Religion.

The Covenant and the Heart

The Covenant is a spiritual reality.

The soul, as mentioned earlier, proceeds from God, and is destined to return to God. When a human being becomes aware of God and acknowledges the existence of God, a relationship begins between the soul (the divine Reality within us) and the Creator (the divine Reality without). This aspect of the Covenant is the one that relates to us personally – to our spiritual journey. This spiritual journey can be described as the search for certitude.

Although this aspect of the Covenant has been referred to already in the previous section entitled 'The Heart', the passages which follow, from the book *Bahá'u'lláh* by Hasan Balyuzi give us a very useful summary:

'There is a covenant implicit in the act of creation. God loved the creation of man, therefore He created him. But He did more than merely create man. God was a 'Hidden Treasure' and wished to be known. Therefore He created man in the image of His own qualities and attributes. He gave man everything that man needed for the sustaining of his physical life. And He sent His Manifestations from age to age to reveal to him His purpose. God did all that for man, and man in return had to fulfil his part, to abide by his side of the covenant. For every covenant is at least bilateral [has two sides]. *"Love Me that I may love thee,"* says Bahá'u'lláh in *The Hidden Words; "if thou lovest Me not, My love can in no wise reach thee."*... We must know God and love God, and know Him and love Him we must through His Manifestations. This is the first Covenant.' 3

The Covenant and the Messengers of God

This aspect of the Covenant gives us insight into the special station of these Chosen Ones who provide the link between God and humanity.

'The second is the Covenant which God makes with His Manifestations. He chooses Them to be the Revealers of His Own Self, the perfect stainless Mirrors that reflect the complete image of the Godhead, names Them His Best Beloved, makes Them His Vicars on earth, upholds Them in the face of vicious, satanic opposition by the generality of mankind, exalts Them as co-sharers of His power, His might, His dominion, His glory. They in turn have to go forward and accomplish the ministry conferred upon Them, without wavering or abandoning Their trust. They have never turned back, no matter how steep, how tortuous the path has been. It is to Them and to those who follow Them and accept blissfully every affliction for Their sakes that God gives ultimate victory. To Abraham God promised that He would bless His seed. And how blessed that seed has been. From that glorious lineage came Redeemers of mankind: Moses, Jesus, Muhammad, the Báb and Bahá'u'lláh. This Covenant between God and His Manifestations is the second Covenant.' 4 (Balyuzi)

Bahá'u'lláh explains that *"the purpose of God in creating man hath been, and will ever be, to enable him to know his Creator and to attain His Presence."* 5

The Manifestations of God are the means by which we acquire that knowledge of God, and make progress towards the goal of attaining the presence of God, and this is the purpose of our spiritual journey.

The Covenant and Religion

"The third Covenant, which is the crowning glory of the other two Covenants, and their full fruition, is the Covenant which the Manifestation of God makes with the peoples of the world and more particularly with those who bear His name. As long as this Covenant could be subverted and eclipsed, the whole purpose of creation remained but partially fulfilled." 6 (Balyuzi)

In the past, people distorted the teachings of the Manifestations of God, putting forward their own ideas and rituals so much that the simple purity of the original teachings became hidden. This rebellion resulted in divisions within these faiths and eventually to the decline of these religions, as people began to turn away from them. "But" as Mr Balyuzi wrote, "those times are past, and the cycle of fulfilment is now with mankind."

This third aspect of the Covenant is one which we need a deep understanding of. 'Abdu'l-Bahá described the Covenant which Bahá'u'lláh established as *"the fortified fortress of the Cause of God and the firm pillar of the religion of God."* 7

A fortified fortress is a structure which has been reinforced to protect against the severest attack! What attack does this Faith need protecting against?

Before we try and answer that question, let us first look back in history.

What Happened in Previous Religions?

'Abdu'l-Bahá states that: *"In former cycles no distinct Covenant was made in writing by the Supreme Pen; no distinct personage was appointed to be the Standard differentiating falsehood from truth ..."* 8

The following excerpt is taken from one of a series of books on the Revelation of Bahá'u'lláh by Bahá'í scholar Adib Taherzadeh:

"History demonstrates that great differences arose among the followers of each religion soon after the death of its Founder. These differences led to schisms and divisions which have increased with the passage of time."

"That religions have divided into sects is not due to the teachings of their Founders, but rather to the immaturity of their followers ... Even in Islam, the most recent of the older religions, men were not sufficiently mature to receive from Muhammad a firm Covenant, similar to that established by Bahá'u'lláh, a Covenant which would require His followers strictly to follow His Faith without creating division within it." 9

The Covenant Today

The main purpose of the Covenant established by Bahá'u'lláh is to maintain unity, to protect the Faith from division arising from within – created by the followers themselves!

'Abdu'l-Bahá affirms that the Covenant is the one power which *"can conserve the oneness of the Bahá'í world ...."* 10

In this Dispensation, the Covenant preserves unity by protecting the Word of God, and providing continuity of Divine guidance. In the Testament of Bahá'u'lláh, this objective was achieved by His appointment of 'Abdu'l-Bahá to be the Centre of the Covenant. In the Will and Testament of 'Abdu'l-Bahá, it was achieved by the establishment of two distinct institutions: the Guardianship and the Universal House of Justice.

Distinguishing Characteristics of the Bahá'í Revelation

The Covenant of Bahá'u'lláh is unique because:

- He wrote down explicitly who would succeed Him after His passing.
- He wrote down how His Faith would be organised as it developed – He laid the foundation of the Administrative Order.
- The language He used was clear and emphatic, leaving no room for doubt.
- It was supported by detailed explanations, laws, principles and guidance.
- The appointment in writing of someone to be the Centre of the Covenant, divinely guided and authorised to interpret the Words of the Manifestation of God is something entirely new in religious history.
- 'Abdu'l-Bahá, the Centre of His Covenant, provided for protection of the

Word and continuity of Divine guidance in His own Will and Testament, by establishing the Guardianship and the Universal House of Justice.
- In this Dispensation, Bahá'u'lláh has promised that mankind will leave behind the stages of childhood and adolescence and attain to its maturity.

The following explanation of the Covenant is taken from a letter of the Universal House of Justice to an individual:

> *"There is also the Lesser Covenant that a Manifestation of God makes with His followers that they will accept His appointed successor after Him. If they do so, the Faith can remain united and pure. If not, the Faith becomes divided and its force spent."*
>
> *"It is a Covenant of this kind that Bahá'u'lláh made with His followers regarding 'Abdu'l-Bahá, and that 'Abdu'l-Bahá perpetuates through the Administrative Order that Bahá'u'lláh had already created. The Covenant of Bahá'u'lláh however is unique in religious history because it was made clearly and explicitly in writing. Therefore, although individuals have broken the Covenant and thus excluded themselves from the community of the Faithful, they have never succeeded in destroying the Covenant itself: it remains inviolable and is the fulfilment of the prophecy that this is the Day that shall not be followed by Night."* 11

If anyone should ask you, "What distinguishes the Bahá'í Revelation from previous Revelations?" you should refer them to the words of the beloved Guardian:

> *"Unlike the Dispensation of Christ, unlike the Dispensation of Muhammad, unlike all the Dispensations of the past, the apostles of Bahá'u'lláh in every land, wherever they labour and toil, have before them in clear, in unequivocal and emphatic language, all the laws, the regulations, the principles, the institutions, the guidance, they require for the prosecution and consummation of their task. Both in the administrative provisions of the Bahá'í Dispensation, and in the matter of succession, as embodied in the twin institutions of the House of Justice and of the Guardianship, the followers of Bahá'u'lláh can summon to their aid such irrefutable evidences of Divine Guidance that none can resist, that none can belittle or ignore. Therein lies the distinguishing feature of the Bahá'í Revelation. Therein lies the strength of the unity of the Faith, of the validity of a Revelation that claims not to destroy or belittle previous Revelations, but to connect, unify, and fulfill them. This is the reason why Bahá'u'lláh and 'Abdu'l-Bahá have both revealed and even insisted upon certain details*

in connection with the Divine Economy which they have bequeathed to us, their followers. This is why such an emphasis has been placed in their Will and Testament upon the powers and prerogatives of the ministers of their Faith.

For nothing short of the explicit directions of their Book, and the surprisingly emphatic language with which they have clothed the provisions of their Will, could possibly safeguard the Faith for which they have both so gloriously laboured all their lives." 12

So powerful is His Covenant, that Bahá'u'lláh's community has safely maintained its unity and has continued to grow from strength to strength for well over a hundred years now. The authors of *The Power of the Covenant* series (National Spiritual Assembly of the Bahá'ís of Canada) observed that:

" ...There is no other great movement in all recorded history – religious, political or social – that has met this universal test ..." 13

Why did the provisions of the Covenant need to be so specific, so explicit?
This was due to our weakness. 'Abdu'l-Bahá wrote:

"Were it not for the protecting power of the Covenant to guard the impregnable fort of the Cause of God, there would arise among the Bahá'ís, in one day, a thousand different sects as was the case in former ages." 14

Why the need for a divinely appointed interpreter?

" ...*so that no one may interpret or explain the religion of God according to his own view or opinion and thus create a sect founded upon his individual understanding of the divine words."* 15

Relating the Covenant to the Individual

The importance of our understanding these various aspects of the Covenant is revealed in the following passages from the Writings of 'Abdu'l-Bahá:

"Today no soul has any station or enjoys any title except the soul who is firm in the Covenant and steadfast in the Testament, who entirely forgets himself and is released from the world." 16

43

> *"Be ye assured with the greatest assurance that, verily, God will help those who are firm in His Covenant in every matter, through His confirmation and favour, the lights of which will shine forth unto the east of the earth, as well as the west thereof. He will make them the signs of guidance among the creation and as shining and glittering stars from all horizons."* 17

Keeping Our Thoughts on the Spiritual Kingdom

To live is to be tested, and the Writings suggest that tests and difficulties are to be welcomed, for if we are not tested, we shall not grow ... and if we maintain our spiritual focus throughout such tests, we will remain happy.

'Abdu'l-Bahá said:

> *"All these examples are to show you that the trials which beset our every step, all our sorrow, pain, shame and grief, are born in the world of matter; whereas the spiritual Kingdom never causes sadness. A man living with his thoughts in this Kingdom knows perpetual joy. The ills all flesh is heir to do not pass him by, but they only touch the surface of his life, the depths are calm and serene."* 18

We have read how attachment to the things of this world can give rise to apathy and lethargy. The Guardian warned that if we become attached to this materialistic civilization, it will absorb our energy and interest so much, that we will end up neglecting our spiritual needs. Even pre-occupation with our work and the day-to-day routine of our physical existence can quite gradually, and without our noticing it, begin to exclude the spiritual exercises so vital to the development of the soul. Then maybe one day .... we are no longer active members of the Bahá'í community, no longer praying, no longer teaching, no longer even trying to live the Bahá'í way of life. This could happen to anyone, and serves to remind us that whatever threatens our spiritual development should be regarded as something which threatens life itself.

 ## The Importance of Remaining Firm in the Covenant

The Guardian identifies the prevailing atmosphere in the world around us as posing one of the greatest threats to our remaining spiritually steadfast:

> *"People are so markedly lacking in spirituality these days that the Bahá'ís should consciously guard themselves against being caught in what one might call the undertow of materialism and atheism, sweeping the world these days. Skepticism, cynicism, disbelief, immorality and hard-heartedness are rife, and as the friends are those who stand for the antithesis of all these things they should beware lest the atmosphere of the present world affects them without their being conscious of it."* [19]

Prayer is essential to remaining steadfast. A famous early Bahá'í called Hájí Mírzá Haydar-'Alí is recorded as saying to a companion:

> "If you really love me, pray that I will die steadfast in the Covenant .... you cannot imagine how very cunning and insidious the self can be. It accompanies a man to the edge of the grave. The only thing that protects us from its deadly grasp is the divine assistance which is granted through prayer." [20]

Being firm in the Covenant in the face of these tests means:
- Remaining alert to the importance of taking care of our spiritual needs as well.
- Reminding ourselves every day, that our spiritual life is most important, that trying to live our lives according to His Teachings and making sincere efforts to teach His Cause in effect prepares us for life in the spiritual worlds of God.
- Feeding your soul by praying and reading the Writings every morning and evening.
- Remaining active. Overcoming feelings of apathy, and performing some form of service for the Faith. To act on our faith, on our beliefs, is the greatest way that we can demonstrate our firmness in the Covenant.

'Abdu'l-Bahá states:

> *"Without action nothing in the material world can be accomplished, neither can words unaided advance a man in the spiritual Kingdom."* [21]

> *"By faith is meant, first, conscious knowledge, and second, the practice of good deeds."* [22]

Covenant-Breaking

Covenant-breaking, although rarely encountered, is a phenomenon of a far more serious nature arising from within a Bahá'í community.

Although this subject is covered in greater detail in the final section of this booklet, the following notes should provide a useful summary of the general principles involved.

The importance of the principle of unity

As discussed previously, one of the most important aspects of the Covenant is its power to maintain the unity of the Faith of Bahá'u'lláh. Unity is the most crucial, central, pivotal and essential principle of His faith. It is an integral, inseparable element of God's religion, and the existence of such a Covenant as He has established, guarantees that His Faith will remain undivided.

How important is this principle? Shoghi Effendi affirms that:

> *"Of the principles enshrined in these Tablets the most vital of them all is the principle of the oneness and wholeness of the human race, which may well be regarded as the hall-mark of Bahá'u'lláh's Revelation and the pivot of His teachings. Of such cardinal importance is this principle of unity that it is expressly referred to in the Book of His Covenant, and He unreservedly proclaims it as the central purpose of His Faith. 'We, verily,' He declares, 'have come to unite and weld together all that dwell on earth.'"* [23]

He again emphasised the importance of the principle of unity when he described *"...the oneness of the entire human race"* as *"the pivotal principle and fundamental doctrine of the Faith..."* [24]

The World as a Patient

Bahá'u'lláh likens the world to a human body which, He says, has been *"afflicted, through various causes, with grave disorders and maladies"* [25]

and he develops this analogy by stating that *"the Prophets of God should be regarded as physicians whose task is to foster the well-being of the world and its peoples..."* [26]

He then reveals:

> "*The All-Knowing Physician hath His finger on the pulse of mankind. He perceiveth the disease, and prescribeth, in His unerring wisdom, the remedy. Every age hath its own problem, and every soul its particular aspiration. The remedy the world needeth in its present-day afflictions can never be the same as that which a subsequent age may require.*" 27

The Prescription

Then what, you may ask, is Bahá'u'lláh's prescription for the body of the world today?

Bahá'u'lláh states that: "*The well-being of mankind, its peace and security, are unattainable unless and until its unity is firmly established.*" 28

What the world needs now, Bahá'u'lláh says, is unity. Every other system has been tried. Wars have been fought, conferences have been held, treaties have been established, systems of government have been tested, and economic plans have been devised. All have failed. Only one solution remains – a spiritual solution, operating through the vehicle of an Administrative Order whose foundations have been established by the Messenger of God Himself.

Writing of religion as a social force, Bahá'u'lláh said:

> "*Religion is the greatest of all means for the establishment of order in the world ...*" 29

> "*That which the Lord hath ordained as the sovereign remedy and mightiest instrument for the healing of all the world is the union of all its peoples in one universal Cause, one common Faith.*" 30

Unity – the Yardstick

The essential point to this, is that the faith that brings together all the peoples of the world must remain undivided. If it does not, then the goals will never be achieved. The stakes are enormous.

The healing of the world, the establishment of order, the solving of the universal problems currently facing the planet: all these depend entirely on the preservation of unity within His Faith – and the preservation of unity is one of the primary responsibilities of the Centre of the Faith. This responsibility was first laid upon Bahá'u'lláh's eldest son 'Abdu'l-Bahá, the Centre of His Covenant, and then in turn passed on to the twin Institutions of the Guardianship and the Universal House of Justice as appointed specifically in 'Abdu'l-Bahá's Will and Testament.

This then, the preservation of unity, is the yardstick which is used to determine whether or not certain actions fall under the category of Covenant-breaking.

The Nature of Covenant-Breaking

In order to break a covenant or agreement, it follows that one had to have entered into it in the first place.

In other words, Covenant-breakers were once members of the Bahá'í community. Most instances of Covenant-breaking have involved individuals challenging the authority of the Centre of the Faith in various ways aimed at undermining the Faith, dividing the community and inducing other members of the community to follow their lead. When it becomes clear that such people are knowingly and deliberately threatening the unity of the Faith, they are counselled, warned and asked to desist from such activities. If they choose to ignore this counsel and continue to show wilful disobedience to the Centre of the Faith, they then risk being expelled from the community. Only the head of the Faith (in this day, the Universal House of Justice) has the authority to declare someone a Covenant-breaker. This is a very rare occurrence. In the few instances where it does happen, members of Bahá'í communities, in accordance with the instructions of Bahá'u'lláh Himself, avoid contact with those that are identified as Covenant-breakers. This ensures that the divisive strategies and negative attitudes which these people display will not further undermine the unity of the Bahá'í community involved. After all, we are all members of this Faith by an act of our own free will. Those who choose to oppose this doctrine of unity alienate themselves from the Faith. We have voluntarily come together because we believe Bahá'u'lláh is the Messenger of God for this day, and we wish to follow His Teachings in their entirety – including His instructions on maintaining unity.

SUMMARY

The Covenant is a spiritual reality. It is a great power, which encompasses and affects everything. All the forces of the universe serve the Covenant.

There are many aspects to the Covenant. The physical universe, the Messengers of God, religion and each individual – every one and every thing has a relationship to the Covenant.

Our **personal obligation to the Covenant** is to come to know God and love God through His Messengers. This spiritual journey can be described as the search for certitude.

The Covenant of Bahá'u'lláh is like **a fortified fortress.** It maintains the unity, shielding the Faith against division arising from within.

The **distinguishing feature of His Covenant** is that it was clearly written down:

- He wrote down explicitly who would succeed Him after His passing.
- He wrote down how His Faith would be organised as it developed – He laid the foundation of the Administrative Order.
- The language He used was clear and emphatic, leaving no room for doubt.
- It was supported by detailed explanations, laws, principles and guidance.
- The appointment in writing of someone to be the Centre of the Covenant, divinely guided and authorised to interpret the Words of the Manifestation of God is something entirely new in religious history.
- 'Abdu'l-Bahá, the Centre of His Covenant, provided for protection of the Word and continuity of Divine guidance in His own written Will and Testament, by establishing the Guardianship and the Universal House of Justice.

To be firm in the Covenant is to be forgetful of self, and to act in faith.

Being firm in the Covenant attracts the assistance of God.

Fixing our thoughts on the spiritual kingdom keeps us happy in difficult times and shields us from becoming caught up in the prevailing atmosphere of the world around us.

4 • THE ADMINISTRATIVE ORDER

As with the subject of the Covenant, it is not possible to cover the Administrative Order in great detail, since it would require an entire book in itself.

We shall nevertheless look briefly at some aspects of it which will enable us to appreciate the central position it occupies in the whole picture of the Bahá'í Revelation.

The Main Characteristic of the Formative Age

With the passing of Bahá'u'lláh and the Centre of His Covenant ('Abdu'l-Bahá), the reins of authority passed to the Guardian (Shoghi Effendi) and the Universal House of Justice, as named in the Will and Testament of 'Abdu'l-Bahá. This transfer of authority also signalled the end of the Heroic Age and the birth of the Formative Age of the Faith. The Heroic Age was associated with the Revelation of the Word of God and the outpouring of Divine guidance to mankind through the ministries of the Báb, Bahá'u'lláh and 'Abdu'l-Bahá. The main characteristic of the Formative Age, however, is the development of the Administrative Order of the Faith, leading eventually to a divine system of Government, containing laws and principles which will be a pattern for future society and the means of unifying the world.

The Bahá'í System – Channelling Spiritual Power

Unlike any previous form of organisation in human society, the Bahá'í system of government has been designed to function with a strong spiritual component.

In previous cycles, when the Manifestation of God passed away, no means existed to contain and channel the spiritual powers which had been released, to ensure that the religion of God went forward, focused and unified to fulfil its God-given potential. This, however, is the very thing that distinguishes this Faith from any that has gone before. The Covenant of Bahá'u'lláh effectively channelled these tremendous spiritual energies while at the same time protecting and maintaining the purity of the Teachings.

Firstly, 'Abdu'l-Bahá became the channel for and protector of these spiritual forces. Then, in His Will and Testament He passed on this responsibility to the Guardian and the Universal House of Justice. In other words, the powers released by Bahá'u'lláh, those awesome, formidable spiritual forces, are today contained and channelled through the Administrative Institutions of the Faith.

The Guardian called it *"the System designed to incarnate the soul of His Faith,"* [1] and described the birth of the Administrative Order in this way:

> *"The moment had now arrived for that undying, that world-vitalizing Spirit ... to incarnate itself in institutions designed to canalize its outspreading energies and stimulate its growth."* [2]

> *" ... this healing Agency, this leavening Power, this cementing Force, intensely alive and all-pervasive, has been taking shape, is crystallizing into institutions ... "* [3]

> *"... it is a perfect form which must be animated by the spirit of the Cause. It is the ideal instrument to make spiritual laws function properly in the material affairs of this world."* [4]

> *"... the Spirit breathed by Bahá'u'lláh upon the world ... can never permeate and exercise an abiding influence upon mankind unless and until it incarnates itself in a visible Order, which would bear His Name, wholly identify itself with His principles, and function in conformity with His laws."* [5]

This visible Order is essentially a divinely conceived merging of Form and Spirit.

Divine Authority Expressed as Love

The authority contained in the persons of Bahá'u'lláh and 'Abdu'l-Bahá was experienced by the believers living in those times as the love of God.

Even those who were not followers were deeply affected not only by the love, but also by the power and authority radiating from their persons. *'It captivated hearts and transformed character.'* [6]

Bahá'u'lláh referred to such transformations in *The Book of Certitude*:

> "These same people ... as soon as they drank the immortal draught of faith, from the cup of certitude, at the hand of the Manifestation of the All-Glorious, were so transformed that they would renounce for His sake their kindred, their substance, their lives, their beliefs, yea, all else save God! So overpowering was their yearning for God, so uplifting their transports of ecstatic delight, that the world and all that is therein faded before their eyes into nothingness." 7

The central figures of the Faith were, during their lifetimes, the focus of the believers' relationship to the Cause of God. During the ministries of the Báb and Bahá'u'lláh, thousands sacrificed their lives for the Centre of the Faith. During the ministry of 'Abdu'l-Bahá, the friends left their homelands, pioneering to distant countries in response to His *Tablets of the Divine Plan* as indeed they did in the time of the Guardian. Their deep love prompted them to make great sacrifices for the sake of the Cause.

Divine Authority Now Expressed Through Institutions

Today, although we no longer have one central figure at the Centre of the Faith, yet the spirit of Bahá'u'lláh lives on, 'intensely alive' within the divinely ordained Institutions of the Administrative Order, namely the Universal House of Justice, the National Spiritual Assemblies and the Local Spiritual Assemblies.

If we are mindful of that spirit, our attitude towards these institutions will be characterized by such qualities as love, respect, obedience and willingness to sacrifice – qualities exemplified so powerfully by the early Bahá'ís in their lives of service to the central figures of the Faith.

We live in a society where many people have negative attitudes towards institutions which are perceived to be wielding power and authority. In such an environment of suspicion, the attitude we Bahá'ís show towards the Institutions of our Faith should be such as to distinguish this community from all others.

The importance of this principle was made very strongly by the Guardian himself in a lengthy letter to the National Spiritual Assembly of Australia and New

Zealand in 1949. The following excerpt is taken from that letter:

> *"The Administrative Order – the Ark destined to preserve its integrity and carry it to safety – must without delay, without exception, claim the attention of the members of this community, its ideals must be continually cherished in their hearts, its purposes studied and kept constantly before their eyes, its requirements wholeheartedly met, its laws scrupulously upheld, its institutions unstintingly supported, its glorious mission noised abroad, and its spirit made the sole motivating purpose of their lives.*
>
> *Then, and only then, will this community ... contribute, to a degree unsuspected as yet by its members, its full share to the world-wide establishment of the Faith of Bahá'u'lláh, the emancipation of its Oriental followers, the recognition of its independence, the birth of its World Order and the emergence of that world civilization which that Order is destined to create."* 8

The Emergence of the Principle of Justice

"... These are the appointed days which ye have been yearningly awaiting in the past – the days of the advent of divine justice. Render ye thanks unto God, O ye concourse of believers." 9

While love is still an important ingredient in the expression of divine authority, the far-reaching changes that will take place in the Formative Age of the Faith will not be achieved by love only. With the rapid growth of the Bahá'í community worldwide, the divine authority at the heart of the Faith has developed a different emphasis: Justice. The emergence of the principle of justice is in response to the needs of society. In the early stages of the development of the Faith, before its emergence from obscurity into the consciousness of the wider community, the need for the application of justice was not so apparent. Now, however, the Bahá'í institutions are poised to take on the role for which they were created – administrators of justice. In a letter written on his behalf Shoghi Effendi observed:

> *"A God that is only loving or only just is not a perfect God. The divinity has to possess both of these aspects as every father ought to express both in his attitude towards his children. If we ponder a while, we will see that*

53

our welfare can be insured only when both of these divine attributes are equally emphasised and practised." 10

The need in the world today is to achieve unity and peace. The disputes between peoples and the wars between nations require the application of a power that will allow new social relationships to be formed. That power is JUSTICE – the essential feature of His World Order.

Bahá'u'lláh wrote:

"The best beloved of all things in My sight is Justice ... " 11

and further, *"That which traineth the world is Justice, for it is upheld by two pillars, reward and punishment. These two pillars are the sources of life to the world."* 12

And 'Abdu'l-Bahá, referring to justice, said:

"The tent of existence is upheld upon the pillar of justice, and not upon forgiveness. The continuance of mankind depends upon justice and not upon forgiveness." 13

Unity and Peace – the Fruits of Justice

According to the teachings of Bahá'u'lláh, applying the principle of Justice to human affairs will bring about unity.

In fact, He states that:

"The purpose of Justice is the appearance of unity among men." 14

And without unity, Bahá'u'lláh says, peace is impossible.

"The well-being of mankind, its peace and security are unattainable unless and until its unity is firmly established." 15

On this matter, the Universal House of Justice has observed:

" ... most people take the opposite point of view: they look upon unity as an ultimate, almost unattainable goal and concentrate first on remedying all the other ills of mankind. If they did but know it, these other ills are but various symptoms and side effects of the basic disease – disunity." 16

Building Divine Government – How Challenging Is That?

The Administrative Order that Bahá'u'lláh has come to establish rests entirely on the creative Word, which establishes the authority of its institutions, guarantees continuity of divine guidance, calls forth power and initiative from the individual and cherishes in its heart the principle of the oneness of mankind.

Eventually, it will produce something that humanity has never before experienced: true theocracy – that is, rule by the Will of God.

> *"It implies,"* the Guardian states, *"an organic change in the structure of present-day society, a change such as the world has not yet experienced."*

> *"It represents the consummation of human evolution ... "* 17

To some people, the idea of changing the structure of present-day society may appear very difficult if not impossible; however, this prize will gradually be won, through constant, patient effort.

> *"..nothing whatsoever,"* 'Abdu'l-Bahá assures us, *"can be regarded as unattainable."* 18

Spiritual Assemblies, the institutions of the Administrative Order, are difficult to establish, primarily because they are designed to operate according to spiritual principles, and this is something entirely new to human experience. We are called upon to put aside all of our own ideas and notions of how we think they should work, and base our understanding on thorough study of the guidance contained in the Word of God. The more we succeed in doing that, the better the results will be.

Shoghi Effendi once likened Bahá'í Administration to a laboratory, where Bahá'ís put into practice the knowledge gained from the Teachings. As Spiritual Assemblies constitute the main framework of Bahá'í Administration, it follows that the meetings of the Spiritual Assemblies will be one of the most vital situations where Bahá'ís work at applying spiritual laws and principles to human affairs. Through the life-giving influence of the Covenant of Bahá'u'lláh, these Assemblies are destined to gradually develop into complex, highly evolved institutions which will reflect the maturation of society.

How important is this process of growth?
The Guardian wrote:
> *"It is this building process, slow and unobtrusive, to which the life of the world-wide Bahá'í Community is wholly consecrated, that constitutes the one hope of a stricken society. For this process is actuated by the generating influence of God's changeless Purpose, and is evolving within the framework of the Administrative Order of His Faith."* 19

Can we influence the rate at which the Faith grows?
The Guardian observed:
> *"One of the main reasons why the Faith does not advance more rapidly is because the friends have not learned to live with, and work within, the framework of the Administrative Order. Either they crystallize it into too set a form, or they rebel against what they feel to be a System, and do not give it sufficient support. Both of these extremes impede the progress of the Faith, and the efficiency of the believers."* 20

The Principle of Obedience

As the Spiritual Assemblies mature and assume greater responsibilities in regard to guidance of the community, the principle of obedience to them will become increasingly important.

We might recognize Bahá'u'lláh and believe in Him, but ultimately, the quality of our faith will be reflected in our attitude, and in our willingness to follow His laws, obey the institutions of His Order and to try living a life according to the teachings and principles of His Faith. As stated earlier, for Bahá'ís, the two principles of recognition and obedience are tied together. By contrast, in the wider society, many people are suspicious of any institution which calls for absolute obedience.

This is understandable, since in recent times there have been many examples of the mis-use of power by dictators, leaders of religious communities and others in positions of authority. A discussion on the question of obedience can be found in *The Covenant of Bahá'u'lláh,* by Bahá'í scholar Adib Taherzadeh. This excerpt is taken from his book:

> "Most of these people are honest thinkers who have come as a result of

their bitter experience to denounce the doctrine of obedience to the teachings of a religion.... . On the other hand, man in his daily life wholeheartedly obeys the directive of individuals or institutions that speak with the voice of truth. He is willing to accept authority which is credible and trustworthy in his view. For instance, a motorist will unhesitatingly follow the sign-post on a road until he reaches his destination. This blind following is due to his faith in the authority of the body which has set up the signposts. Similarly, a patient will willingly allow a surgeon to operate on a cancerous growth because he has faith in his diagnosis. There will be a similar response if one recognizes the truth of the Cause of God. Once recognized as credible, obedience to the teachings will not be difficult to achieve." [21]

Practising Obedience

On the face of it, people appear to have no trouble with the concept of obedience to God, but in practice, when asked to demonstrate obedience to Spiritual Assemblies, there is a tendency among some to disregard a fundamental principle.

Rather than viewing the Spiritual Assembly as an institution ordained by God, obedience to which signifies our obedience to God, they focus instead on the human face of the Assembly and assume that since the individuals on it are flawed, that its judgement will be similarly flawed. In this connection, Shoghi Effendi wrote:

> " ... there is a distinction of fundamental importance which should be always remembered in this connection, and this is between the Spiritual Assembly as an institution, and the persons who compose it. These are by no means supposed to be perfect, nor can they be considered as being **inherently** superior to the rest of their fellow-believers. It is precisely because they are subject to the same human limitations that characterize the other members of the community that they have to be elected every year. The existence of elections is a sufficient indication that Assembly members, though forming part of an institution that is divine and perfect, are nevertheless themselves imperfect. But this does not necessarily imply that their judgement is defective. For as 'Abdu'l-Bahá has repeatedly emphasized Bahá'í Assemblies are under the guidance and protection of God. " [22]

The True Source of Law

Law is the basis of society because it brings order to human affairs.

'Abdu'l-Bahá revealed:

> "Briefly, the supreme Manifestations of God are aware of the reality of the mysteries of beings. Therefore, They establish laws which are suitable and adapted to the state of the world of man, for religion is the essential connection which proceeds from the realities of things .... The Prophets of God, the supreme Manifestations, are like skilled physicians, and the contingent world is like the body of man: the divine laws are the remedy and treatment." 23

When people in their hearts really believe in laws, then they will obey them. This obedience transforms society and causes the progress of humanity. This is why religion is the real source of law, because the Revelation of God affects the hearts of men and brings these attributes out. Obedience to the laws of God is the means to developing the spiritual side of our nature – our true selves. Bahá'u'lláh wrote:

> "True loss is for him whose days have been spent in utter ignorance of his self." 24

> "And be ye not like those who forget God, and whom He hath therefore caused to forget their own selves." 25

In the series of booklets entitled *Power of the Covenant* (National Spiritual Assembly of Canada), the authors point out that: 'Repeatedly in all the holy Scriptures the human heart or conscience is referred to as the "earth". It is only the Revelation of God which can drive the roots of law deep into this earth. Unless the roots of the laws and institutions of a community are firmly embedded in the hearts of the mass of the people, the social order cannot survive.' 26

The Flow of Divine Authority

Shoghi Effendi clearly shows that acknowledging the flow of authority from Bahá'u'lláh through 'Abdu'l-Bahá and then to the Guardian and the Universal House of Justice is an essential ingredient to becoming firm in the Covenant.

Further, he links order to obedience:

> "*An intellectual grasp of the Teachings is purely superficial; with the first real test such believers are shaken from the bough! But once a Bahá'í has the profound conviction of the authority from God, vested in the Prophet, passed on to the Master, and by Him, to the Guardians, and which flows out through the Assemblies and creates order based on obedience – once a Bahá'í has this, nothing can shake him ...*" 27

As the spirit of faith grows within us, our understanding of the principle of obedience will also grow, and we will begin to appreciate the spiritual nature of the laws revealed by God, and to discover their purpose. Referring to His Book of Laws, the *Kitáb-i-Aqdas*, Bahá'u'lláh says:

> "*Think not that We have revealed unto you a mere code of laws. Nay, rather, We have unsealed the choice Wine with the fingers of might and power.*" 28

Separating Principles from Personalities

Since Spiritual Assemblies* are the elected bodies charged with administering the affairs of the community, they must inevitably make decisions which affect both the community as a whole, and individuals within it.

How effective these institutions are, and how rapidly they mature and develop depends largely on the attitude of the individual Bahá'ís towards them. The divinely ordained institution of the Spiritual Assembly is here to stay, whereas those serving on them will come and go. If we look at the people we elect to serve on these Assemblies, and allow our feelings about their personal failings or shortcomings to colour our view of the institution as a whole, then there is no doubt that such an attitude will hold back the progress of the Cause in that place. In this regard, Shoghi Effendi stated:

> "*Another thing he wants the young people to do is to set an example in obedience to the Administration, and to rise above the tendency, alas, so pronounced in some of the friends, to consider personalities instead of principles. This Cause is based on spiritual laws, and we must consider these, and obey them, and not lose time in thinking about the individual person's peculiarities, or opinions ...*" 29

[*At this early stage in their development, the local and national institutions of the Faith are referred to as Spiritual Assemblies. In time, as they mature, they will assume their proper titles – Houses of Justice. The Universal House of Justice and the Local House of Justice were both ordained by Bahá'u'lláh in the *Kitáb-i-Aqdás*. The institution of the National or 'Secondary' House of Justice was established by 'Abdu'l-Bahá in His Will and Testament.]

The System Is Perfect (we are not)

In many places through his writings, Shoghi Effendi stressed the need for patience with regard to the workings of the Administrative Order, as we are all still learning how it functions and how to use it correctly:

> *"The Bahá'ís are far from perfect, as individuals or when they serve on elected bodies, but the system of Bahá'u'lláh is perfect and gradually the believers will mature and the system will work better."* 30

Spiritual Conference

Those of you who have observed or listened to the way issues are debated in the political arena of this country (and many others), will agree that it is a process which seems to bring out some of the worst traits in people – seemingly encouraging the lower nature.

In contrast to this, one of the distinguishing features of the Bahá'í Administrative Order is that it was designed to allow us to express our spiritual natures through the art of consultation. 'Abdu'l-Bahá even went so far as to lay down spiritual pre-conditions for the process of consultation.

First, *"absolute love and harmony"* amongst those consulting, and secondly that they should turn to God and beseech His aid. He goes on to say, *"They must then proceed with the utmost devotion, courtesy, dignity, care and moderation to express their views."* 31

Observing these pre-conditions will, as 'Abdu'l-Bahá predicted, lead to: "... *spiritual conference and not the mere voicing of personal views ...*" 32 Consultation, however, is not about sameness. On the contrary, just as the various instruments of an orchestra playing in harmony create wonderful music, consultation in its best form expresses the great diversity of those participating in it. Bahá'í scholar Marzieh Gail writes:

> "True Bahá'í consultation is something to remember. In those moments when we, groping toward the techniques of the future, experience collective harmony – when we become, briefly, a composite reflection of spiritual light – the world is a lovely place to be in. Perhaps to the amateur, pleasure results when a committee reaches harmony because of the members' similarity to one another; to the connoisseur, however, the real joy of harmony is only reached when dissimilarities are at work together – when opposites are reconciled – when tension is balanced, poised, distributed." 33

Finding the Balance Between Form and Spirit

It is clear that the Guardian considered this matter to be of vital importance. In his outstanding letter of 27 February 1929 titled 'The World Order of Bahá'u'lláh', in the space of a single paragraph, he mentions this principle three times:

> " *I need not dwell upon what I have already reiterated and emphasized that the administration of the Cause is to be conceived as an instrument and not a substitute for the Faith of Bahá'u'lláh, that it should be regarded as a channel through which His promised blessings may flow, that it should guard against such rigidity as would clog and fetter the liberating forces released by His Revelation.*"

> "*... that the whole machinery of assemblies, of committees and conventions is to be regarded as a means, and not an end in itself ...* "

> " *... to prayerfully watch lest the tool should supersede the Faith itself, lest undue concern for the minute details arising from the administration of the Cause obscure the vision of its promoters ...* " 34

This need to guard against the tendency in Bahá'í communities to develop Form (administrative procedures) to the point where it stifles the Spirit is a theme which we see appearing again and again throughout Shoghi Effendi's writings. Here are a further selection of excerpts from letters written on his behalf.

"*The need is very great, everywhere in the world, in and outside the Faith, for a true spiritual awareness to pervade and motivate peoples' lives. No amount of administrative procedure or adherence to rules can take the place of this soul-characteristic, this spirituality which is the essence of Man. He is very glad to see you are stressing this and aiding the friends to realize its supreme importance."* 35

"*The friends must never mistake the Bahá'í administration for an end in itself. It is merely the instrument of the spirit of the Faith."* 36

"*Administrative efficiency and order should always be accompanied by an equal degree of love, of devotion and of spiritual development. Both of them are essential and to attempt to dissociate one from the other is to deaden the body of the Cause. In these days, when the Faith is still in its infancy, great care must be taken lest mere administrative routine stifles the spirit which must feed the body of the Administration itself. That spirit is its propelling force and the motivating power of its very life."* 37

"*So often young communities, in their desire to administer the Cause, lose sight of the fact that these spiritual relationships are far more important and fundamental than the rules and regulations which must govern the conduct of Community affairs."* 38

The final excerpt is from *Trustees of the Merciful* by Adib Taherzadeh:

"A deeper study of the writings of Shoghi Effendi on Bahá'í Administration will enable the individual to realise that the aim of the members of the Assembly in this period of the Formative Age of the Faith should not primarily be directed towards becoming efficient administrators or specialists in solving the community's various complex problems but rather towards creating a spiritual atmosphere during the course of their meetings, so that the confirmations of Bahá'u'lláh may reach them from every direction and that, through His assistance, they may be able to resolve their problems." 39

The Value of a Visible Example

Being an example involves more than just having a strong belief or faith – it also requires us, as individuals, to demonstrate good character.

In a letter written on his behalf the Guardian stated:

> "There is a difference between character and faith; it is often very hard to accept this fact and put up with it, but the fact remains that a person may believe in and love the Cause – even to being ready to die for it – and yet not have a good personal character, or possess traits at variance with the teachings. We should try to change, to let the Power of God help recreate us and make us true Bahá'ís in deed as well as in belief. But sometimes the process is slow, sometimes it never happens because the individual does not try hard enough. But these things cause us suffering and are a test to us in our fellow-believers, most especially if we love them and have been their teacher!" [40]

Similarly, in a letter written on his behalf in 1946 the Guardian asserted: *"The world is tired of words; it wants example ... "* [41]

Bahá'u'lláh has come to empower us to be an example to the world by establishing a new Order. We, His followers, are in a sense His first citizens in this new world society. We are called upon to show forth those attributes that are the distinguishing characteristics of this new Order – both as individuals, and as a community.

What unique example is required from us Bahá'ís?

The cornerstone of the Faith of Bahá'u'lláh is unity. Its goal is the unity of the entire human race. Therefore, our first and most important task is to demonstrate a spirit of unity which distinguishes us in human society. Just as in the physical world, the greater the force field surrounding the magnet, the more powerfully will it attract – so it is in the spiritual world. The greater the spirit of unity, the greater will be the power of the faith to attract those souls seeking after God.

This spirit is to be expressed through the Administrative Order which, as it begins *"to function with efficiency and vigour,"* will, Shoghi Effendi wrote, *"assert its claim and demonstrate its capacity to be regarded not only as the nucleus but the very pattern of the New World Order destined to embrace in the fullness of time the whole of mankind."* [42]

We are being asked to begin the establishment of a global society now! The future world civilisation will be shaped on the framework we are building today. The eradication of prejudice, the full expression of the equality of women and men and the establishment of a new social order are just some of the ideals we are working to achieve. When we stop to think about what we are aiming for, we quickly realise that only a power born of God could cause ordinary people all over the world to attempt so many diverse and challenging goals all at once!

SUMMARY

The main characteristic of the Formative Age of the Faith is the development of the Administrative Order. This Administrative Order will lead eventually to a divine system of Government, having laws and principles which will be a pattern for future society. It will provide the means of unifying the world.

It is a system designed to function with a **strong spiritual component.** In other words, the Administration is not an end in itself – it is merely a form which facilitates the flow of spirit. Administrative routine should not be allowed to stifle that spirit. Our attitude towards the Institutions of this Administrative Order needs to be **characterised by love and a willingness to sacrifice.** Such an attitude should distinguish the Bahá'í community from others in which people generally have a negative and distrustful view of those in authority.

The **role of Spiritual Assemblies will gradually evolve to meet the needs of society.** These Spiritual Assemblies were in fact created to administer Justice, and in time they will be properly called Houses of Justice. The purpose of Justice is to bring unity and peace to mankind.

Building a divine system of government will not be easy. It implies gradually changing the structure of present-day society. The potential for such change will increase in proportion to the rate of maturation in Spiritual Assemblies.

Religion is the real source of law, because the Word of God can drive the roots of laws deep into the earth of the human heart or conscience. By being obedient to the laws, we demonstrate our firmness in the Covenant – and this is the means of developing our spiritual nature, our true selves.

4 • THE ADMINISTRATIVE ORDER

Obedience to Spiritual Assemblies is a sign of our obedience to God, and by supporting the Assemblies, we help to hasten their development and maturation.

The **System of Bahá'u'lláh is perfect** – we are not.

True consultation comes about as we express our spiritual natures.

It is vital that we **do not allow administrative routine to stifle the spirit of the Faith,** but rather, concentrate on creating a spiritual atmosphere in our meetings. The Administration is a means, not an end in itself.

The pattern of community life we are establishing now is the **framework for a future world civilisation** envisaged by Bahá'u'lláh. We are, in a sense, His first citizens in this new world society.

The world is tired of words. Our task as a Bahá'í community is to demonstrate a spirit of unity which will be expressed through the proper functioning of the Administrative Order. That is how we will increase our spirituality, our spiritual magnetism, and attract those souls searching after God.

5 • THE INDIVIDUAL & THE COMMUNITY

Religion has always carried with it the spirit which enables human society to achieve increasingly greater and fuller expressions of unity.

'Abdu'l-Bahá states:

> "*God has sent forth His Prophets for the sole purpose of creating love and unity in the world of human hearts."* 1

Progressively uniting family, then tribe and nation, that spirit now brings with it the power to transform society yet again and create a unified global civilisation. It is in the local community that this power of change first expresses itself.

The existence of continually evolving communities is an essential aspect of the Faith of Bahá'u'lláh. The communities are constantly evolving because they are connected with the power of the Covenant through Spiritual Assemblies – the divinely conceived and divinely guided agencies of His Administrative Order.

The mission of the Faith is to transform human society, and in every community the Bahá'ís are trying to put these ideals to work, transforming principles into practice. This is why becoming involved in community life is so important – why monasticism has been prohibited by Bahá'u'lláh. By each person participating, the Bahá'ís can demonstrate the spirit of love and fellowship that will characterise *"the world religion of the future."* 2

We cannot do this by hiding ourselves away. In a letter to the Bahá'ís of New Zealand in 1957, Shoghi Effendi wrote:

> "*All must participate, whether young or old, veterans as well as newly enrolled believers, all must contribute their share to the ultimate success of this mighty collective enterprise, however limited their means, however modest their abilities, however restricted the range of their previous experiences."* 3

Sacrifice and Sacrifice

Whenever a new Manifestation of God appears, great spiritual forces associated with Their Revelation are released into the world.

Those people who were privileged to live in Bahá'u'lláh's time witnessed potent those spiritual forces were. His followers were utterly transformed, and their love for Him was so great, that they were willing to give up everything for His sake. During the Heroic Age of the Faith, thousands who accepted and acknowledged the truth of this Revelation found themselves persecuted, or even subjected to cruel torture, and killed for their faith. Through their death, they proclaimed the birth of a new religion. Today, in this the Formative Age of the Faith we also are being asked to sacrifice ourselves, but in a different way. 'Abdu'l-Bahá stated:

> "Sacrifice of life is of two kinds. To be killed for the Cause is not so difficult as to live for it in absolute obedience to the commands of God." 4

And in *The Advent of Divine Justice*, Shoghi Effendi explained:

> "The community ... of the Faith of Bahá'u'lláh in the American continent – the spiritual descendants of the dawn-breakers of an heroic Age, who by their death proclaimed the birth of that Faith – must, in turn, usher in, not by their death but through living sacrifice, that promised World Order, the shell ordained to enshrine that priceless jewel, the world civilization, of which the Faith itself is the sole begetter." 5

The Battleground Within

So this is the real battleground – within each of us!

If we wish to contribute towards achieving a spirit of unity, if we wish to help create harmony, if we wish to make progress on our personal spiritual journey – then we must be prepared to look at ourselves and make personal sacrifices if necessary. This is perhaps one of the most important ways in which we express our firmness in the Covenant as individuals. On this subject, Bahá'í scholar Adib Taherzadeh shared the following:

> "In one of His Tablets 'Abdu'l-Bahá states that the word 'courageous' can apply to a person who conquers his own self and passion. For it is easier to conquer whole countries than to defeat one's own self. The purpose of the coming of the Manifestations of God is to endow the soul of man with spiritual qualities and enable him to defeat his greatest enemy – his own self." 6

In a letter written on his behalf to an individual, the Guardian states:

> "Life is a constant struggle, not only against forces around us, but above all against our own 'ego'." 7

Community life is about balance. The rights of individuals are balanced against the welfare of the group. Personal freedom is balanced against the need to maintain unity, and the key to maintaining unity lies in the willingness to sacrifice. A letter written on the Guardian's behalf counsels us to:

> " ... *curb our individualism when we are confronted with problems and issues affecting the general welfare of the Cause. For Bahá'í community life implies a consciousness of group solidarity strong enough to enable every individual believer to give up what is essentially personal for the sake of the common weal.*" 8

The Power of Unity

The Guardian frequently referred to the magnetic power of unity and not surprisingly, he stated that the *"watchword"* of the new World Order *"is unity."* 9

> "*All the Bahá'ís, new and old alike, should devote themselves as much as possible to teaching the Faith; they should also realize that the atmosphere of true love and unity which they manifest within the Bahá'í Community will directly affect the public, and be the greatest magnet for attracting people to the Faith and confirming them.*" 10

He referred to the unique example of our community life, and indicated that by demonstrating the Bahá'í way of life, we contribute towards "*the fundamental reorganization and the supreme felicity of all mankind.*" 11

And surely, you will experience some of the happiest moments and most memorable times of your life while living in a Bahá'í community and working with fellow Bahá'ís. You may also find that some of the most severe personal tests you face will likewise come from within a community of Bahá'ís.

Such is the power of the individual within the community, that each person can either promote a spirit of unity or hold it back, by his/her actions and attitudes.

Contributing to Unity – a Personal Challenge

The social environment of a Bahá'í community can present us with great personal challenges.

5 • THE INDIVIDUAL AND THE COMMUNITY

Monument of the Greatest Holy Leaf in the Arc Gardens, Haifa

5 • THE INDIVIDUAL AND THE COMMUNITY

It is a testing ground – learning to work together in harmony and practising spiritual consultation are processes which challenge souls! The achievement of a true spirit of unity will depend largely on the attitude of the friends towards each other. In a letter written on his behalf to an individual, Shoghi Effendi offered this advice:

> *"You may be sure he will pray for the unity of the ... believers, as this is of paramount importance, and upon it depends the development of the Cause there, and the success of every teaching effort. The thing the friends need – everywhere – is a greater love for each other, and this can be acquired by greater love for Bahá'u'lláh; for if we love Him deeply enough, we will never allow personal feelings and opinions to hold His Cause back; we will be willing to sacrifice ourselves to each other for the sake of the Faith, and be, as the Master said, one soul in many bodies."* 12

And in the following excerpt, again taken from a letter written on his behalf, we read some of the Guardian's most profound words of advice to the individual:

> *"There is only one remedy for this: to study the administration, to obey the Assemblies, and each believer seek to perfect his own character as a Bahá'í. We can never exert the influence over others which we can exert over ourselves. If we are better, if we show love, patience, and understanding of the weakness of others, if we seek to never criticize but rather encourage, others will do likewise, and we can really help the Cause through our example and spiritual strength. The Bahá'ís everywhere when the administration is first established, find it very difficult to adjust themselves. They have to learn to obey, even when the Assembly may be wrong, for the sake of unity. They have to sacrifice their personalities to a certain extent, in order that the Community life may grow and develop as a whole. These things are difficult, but we must realize that they will lead to a very much greater, more perfect, way of life when the Faith is properly established according to the administration."* 13

The diversity of our communities is one of the greatest assets of the Faith because diversity provides opportunities for growth. God tests His servants continually, and overcoming these tests lies at the heart of the individual's relationship to the Covenant of Bahá'u'lláh. The real struggle for world unity is going on inside Bahá'í communities all around the planet, as we gradually, through trial and error, build the framework of a new model of community living.

> *"The Bahá'í administration is only the first shaping of what in future will come to be the social life and laws of community living. As yet the believers are only first beginning to grasp and practice it properly. So we must*

have patience if at times it seems a little self-conscious and rigid in its workings. It is because we are learning something very difficult but very wonderful – how to live together as a community of Bahá'ís, according to the glorious teachings." 14

And, we must be the first to learn this new system ...

"They must be ever conscious of their supreme duty towards their fellow-men – the duty of holding up to their enquiring gaze the model upon which a sound future society can be constructed. This is the system of Bahá'u'lláh which the Bahá'ís must first learn themselves to live up to, and then share with the whole world." 15

Attitude Is Critical

If we are to benefit in some way from any process of testing, we need to have the right attitude. Otherwise, we may be hurt or become disillusioned and withdraw from community activities.

When we become Bahá'ís, we are so happy. The idea that we might pull back or withdraw from the Bahá'í community at some point, for whatever reason, simply would not occur to us. However, estrangement can happen, and if we are to grow through tests and remain steadfast in the Faith, we will need patience and perseverance. In *Gleanings from the Writings of Bahá'u'lláh*, we read Bahá'u'lláh's own words of advice:

"Sharp must be thy sight, O Dhabíh, and adamant thy soul, and brass-like thy feet, if thou wishest to be unshaken by the assaults of the selfish desires that whisper in men's breasts." 16

The Guardian advocated that we become *"truly firm, deep, spiritually convinced Bahá'ís."* He went on to say: *"An intellectual grasp of the teachings is purely superficial; with the first real test such believers are shaken from the bough! But once a Bahá'í has the profound conviction of the authority from God, vested in the Prophet, passed on to the Master, and by Him, to the Guardians, and which flows out through the assemblies and creates order based on obedience – once a Bahá'í has this, nothing can shake him."* 17

In this condition of certitude, when we are tested, we will experience changes in attitudes, growth in our capabilities, and spiritual happiness and well-being.

5 • THE INDIVIDUAL AND THE COMMUNITY

The sea wall of the prison city of 'Akká

For these reasons, tests are to be looked at positively, because they so quickly strengthen us, and provide for us the means to make great progress on our personal spiritual journey.

The following excerpt shows clearly that the Guardian placed great value on those believers who developed inner strength through overcoming tests:

> "There is always an important difference between friends and tested friends. No matter how precious the first type may be, the future of the Cause rests upon the latter." [18]

And the Master stated:

> "The necessity ... is to be firm in the Cause of God and withstand the hidden and evident tests. Thanks be to God that you are distinguished and made eminent by this blessing. Anybody can be happy in the state of comfort, ease, health, success, pleasure and joy; but if one will be happy and contented in the time of trouble, hardship and prevailing disease, it is the proof of nobility." [19]

We in the West

Having to deal with mental tests – those things which paralyze our spiritual faculties, is something which affects particularly the Bahá'ís of the West, who are immersed in materialistic societies.

The Guardian wrote:

> "Indeed the chief reason for the evils now rampant in society is the lack of spirituality. The materialistic civilization of our age has so much absorbed the energy and interest of mankind that people in general do no longer feel the necessity of raising themselves above the forces and conditions of their daily material existence. There is not sufficient demand for things that we call spiritual to differentiate them from the needs and requirements of our physical existence." [20]

We live in a society where most people are motivated by the desire to achieve material wealth and economic security, and Bahá'ís are not immune to this. When we lose our spiritual focus, how quickly we too fall back into that familiar preoccupation with money and material comfort. How difficult it is to keep focusing on spiritual goals – not allowing material goals to dominate our daily existence. Any number of things can take our attention away from our spiritual life. Most of us can no doubt identify with the following examples identified by Shoghi Effendi: *"personal professional preoccupations"*, and *"the prevailing tendencies in the general thought, sentiment, and manners of the people in whose midst you work ... "* [21]

Which raises the question: How do I stay 'spiritually alive' while also living and working in a spiritually bankrupt society? It is a challenge which each one of us will have to respond to, and highlights the importance of the relationship between the individual and the community. We walk the spiritual path alone, yet there are times when we enjoy spiritual companionship.

Where moral choices and decisions affecting our spiritual life have to be made, we take these steps alone, and the obligations of praying and meditating, reciting one of the obligatory prayers daily, reading the Writings in the morning and evening, and teaching the Faith, we fulfil by our own volition.

However, beyond ourselves, the people we choose to associate with can have a great influence on our spiritual health. Bahá'u'lláh writes:

> *"The company of the ungodly increaseth sorrow, whilst fellowship with the righteous cleanseth the rust from off the heart. He that seeketh to commune with God, let him betake himself to the companionship of His loved ones ... "* [22]

and the Guardian points to the great power within the community itself:

> *"Indeed, the believers have not yet fully learned to draw on each other's strength and consolation in time of need. The Cause of God is endowed with tremendous powers, and the reason the believers do not gain more from it is because they have not learned to draw fully on these mighty forces of love and strength and harmony generated by the Faith."* [23]

It is true, there may be instances when neither the friends nor the Institutions provide the love and support at the time we most need it. Such occasions are a true test of our firmness in the Covenant and of our ability to be radiantly submissive – relying only upon God. In this regard, Bahá'u'lláh has stated:

> *"For every one of you his paramount duty is to choose for himself that on which no other may infringe and none usurp from him. Such a thing – and to this the Almighty is My witness – is the love of God, could ye but perceive it."* [24]

It is this 'love of God' which is the source of true happiness.

Being Happy

There may be times in our life when we feel very happy because everything is going well for us, we are prosperous and the world seems to be smiling on us.

> If however, our happiness becomes dependent on the material world, then it follows that we will quickly become unhappy if things do not go well.

Spiritual happiness, on the other hand, does not depend on the material world. It is, first, a gift from God.

> *"As to spiritual happiness, this is the true basis of the life of man, for life is created for happiness, not for sorrow; for pleasure, not for grief .... This great blessing and precious gift is obtained by man only through the guidance of God ... "* 25

> *"Verily, thy Lord lighteth the lamp of Love in the heart of whomsoever He chooseth. This is indeed the great happiness."* 26

It comes with the love of God.

> *"Spiritual happiness is eternal and unfathomable. This kind of happiness appeareth in one's soul with the love of God and suffereth one to attain to the virtues and perfections of the world of humanity."* 27

In this condition, we are uplifted, our spirits soar, and we feel a mystical connection to our Creator. 'Abdu'l-Bahá further states that *"human happiness is founded upon spiritual behaviour."* 28 Similarly, the Guardian affirms that spirituality can be cultivated, that certain actions have a spiritual effect. He explains:

> *"The spirit of the age, taken on the whole, is irreligious. Man's outlook on life is too crude and materialistic to enable him to elevate himself into the higher realms of the spirit."*

> *"It is this condition, so sadly morbid, into which society has fallen, that religion seeks to improve and transform. For the core of religious faith is that mystic feeling which unites Man with God. This state of spiritual communion can be brought about and maintained by means of meditation and prayer. And this is the reason why Bahá'u'lláh has so much stressed the importance of worship. It is not sufficient for a believer merely to accept and observe the teachings. He should, in addition, cultivate the sense of spirituality which he can acquire chiefly by means of prayer. The Bahá'í Faith, like all other Divine Religions, is thus fundamentally mystic in character. Its chief goal is the development of the individual and society, through the acquisition of spiritual virtues and powers. It is the soul of man which has first to be fed. And this spiritual nourishment prayer can best provide."* 29

5 • THE INDIVIDUAL AND THE COMMUNITY

Window in the Pilgrim House at Bahjí

SUMMARY

Becoming involved is important. It is through everyone participating that we can demonstrate to all people how the power of unity changes the world.

Unity is the most powerful magnet for attracting people to the Faith.

There are **two kinds of sacrifice**; one is giving our lives (as the martyrs have), while the other is living our lives in obedience to the commands of God. It is not by our death, "but through living sacrifice" that we will build the World Order of Bahá'u'lláh.

The real battle is the battle within – conquering our own egos. The Messengers of God came to give us the spiritual qualities to enable us to defeat our greatest enemy – our self.

Community life is about balancing personal freedom against the need to maintain unity. The spirit of sacrifice is what maintains and strengthens the spirit of unity.

Community life can bring personal tests. Learning to work together and practising consultation can be very challenging – it can also be very rewarding and very gratifying. Sometimes we may need to sacrifice our personalities to a certain extent if necessary, and learn to obey the Spiritual Assembly even if it is wrong, for the sake of unity.

Diversity is an asset. It provides opportunities for growth.

The struggle for world unity is going on inside Bahá'í communities, as we work to construct a new model of community living. The Bahá'ís must achieve it first – then we will have something to share with the whole world.

We are called to become **firm, deep, spiritually convinced Bahá'ís**, prepared to be patient and to persevere. Being strong in our faith when things are very difficult is the proof of nobility.

Mental tests can paralyse our spiritual faculties. Mental tests are associated with materialism. We Bahá'ís are not immune to these tests. We have to be alert, and resist the tendency to allow our energy and interest to be entirely absorbed by the occupation with material needs.

We can combat these mental tests by paying attention to our personal spiritual obligations daily, and by drawing on the strength of our fellow Bahá'ís. Prayer and meditation provide the means of cultivating the sense of spirituality.

True and lasting happiness comes with the love of God. Spiritual growth is a response to your service to the Faith – it does not come about through taking out what you feel you need from the Faith.

6 • UNDERSTANDING COVENANT-BREAKING

Covenant-breaking is something which affects the soul.

Should an incidence of Covenant-breaking arise within a Bahá'í community, it is treated very seriously since it threatens the spiritual health of the members of that community.

The idea that somebody might have a spiritual sickness may seem absurd to some people, yet this is how Covenant-breaking is described in the Bahá'í Writings. It is a unique and rare phenomenon, unlike any other form of human behaviour which we may have previously experienced. Even followers of other Faiths will not know of it. The reason that it is not associated with previous religious dispensations is due to the fact that no past religion has had a Covenant like that established by Bahá'u'lláh (see section on Covenant).

Briefly, the Covenant is that spiritual power which enabled this Divine Revelation to remain intact as it made the transition from the care of its Revealer (Bahá'u'lláh) to the Centre of His Covenant ('Abdu'l-Bahá), and finally, from His care into the care of the twin institutions of the Guardianship (Shoghi Effendi) and the Universal House of Justice. It is the key ingredient which will empower this Faith to achieve what has never been achieved before – a unified global society which grows and evolves according to spiritual foundations laid down by the Manifestation of God.

In the past, a few misguided individuals have tried to sever that link which guarantees the Faith's unity, and in spite of counselling and warnings, have persisted in divisive behaviour. This has led to their expulsion from the community by the Head of the Faith and subsequently being described as Covenant-breakers. In a sense they expel themselves, since they choose not to observe the specific instructions of the Head of the Faith with regard to its very basis and foundation. Although it is rare, and most Bahá'ís may never encounter it, it is important to gain an understanding of the nature of Covenant-breaking, by looking briefly at some examples of the actions of Covenant-breakers from the early days of the Faith through to more recent times.

A Brief History

During the ministry of Bahá'u'lláh, Mírzá Yahyá claimed to be the Báb's successor, and a Manifestation of God. He tried to poison Bahá'u'lláh, attempted to organise the assassination of Bahá'u'lláh, spread malicious rumours and tried to divide the community.

During the ministry of 'Abdu'l-Bahá, His half-brother Mírzá Muhammed-'Alí, was intensely jealous of 'Abdu'l-Bahá 's position, rank, knowledge and virtue. He attacked 'Abdu'l-Bahá through verbal abuse and malicious accusations. He launched a conspiracy for the murder of 'Abdu'l-Bahá.

Ibrahim Khayr'u'lláh, a Syrian doctor who joined the Faith in Cairo and was initially much praised by 'Abdu'l-Bahá for his services to the Faith, became a Covenant-breaker through writing booklets against the Master and attempting to induce members of the American Bahá'í community – many of whom were newly declared – into following him rather than 'Abdu'l-Bahá as the Head of the Faith.

During the ministry of Shoghi Effendi, several attacks were made on the Covenant. Ahmad Sohrab, a former secretary of 'Abdu'l-Bahá, attacked the Administrative Order at great length. Ruth White tried to discredit the Administration and questioned the authenticity of the Will and Testament of 'Abdu'l-Bahá; she even went so far as appealing to the civil authorities in Palestine to take legal action over the latter question, a request which the British Authorities rejected.

Avarih, formerly a very active Bahá'í teacher, attacked the Guardian in ten volumes of books. Hermann Zimmer attacked the Faith in a book which again tried to undermine the Will and Testament of 'Abdu'l-Bahá. In 1960, Mason Remey who was at the time a Hand of the Cause, attempted to usurp the Guardianship by claiming to be the next Guardian. Also, all of the closest relatives of the Guardian – his two brothers and two sisters, and all of his cousins, the grandchildren of 'Abdu'l-Bahá – became infected with the spirit of Covenant-breaking and were declared Covenant-breakers.

(Summarised from The Power of the Covenant series – National Spiritual Assembly of Canada)

Are There Different Degrees of Covenant-Breaking?

Clearly not all people who have been identified as Covenant-breakers are guilty of the actions described above. Some people have joined their ranks merely through associating with known Covenant-breakers.

How does this happen? 'Abdu'l-Bahá has described Covenant-breakers as persons who have an infectious spiritual disease. To illustrate this point, he explains how a person with a contagious physical disease who associates with a *"thousand souls, in a short time ... will infect a number of those healthy persons."* 1

Shoghi Effendi used the analogy of leprosy to explain Covenant-breaking:

"If you put a leper in a room with healthy people, he cannot catch their health; on the contrary they are very likely to catch his horrible ailment." 2

Elsewhere he also affirms that Covenant-breakers are *"spiritually sick"* and that contact with them *"exposes one to grave danger of contagion."* 3

This demonstrates how people, merely through association, become infected with the spirit of Covenant-breaking. Interestingly, although it may appear to us that they are more like victims than perpetrators, when it comes to how they are to be treated, no distinction is made. On this subject the House of Justice has clearly written that:

"All Covenant-breakers, regardless of the nature of their disobedience to the Covenant should be treated in exactly the same manner." 4

When the friends have to deal with the presence of Covenant-breakers nearby, these occasions invariably present a personal challenge – a test of their firmness in the Covenant. Some Bahá'ís may be completely taken by surprise, both by the feelings it evokes in them, and the difficulty they have in trying to understand it. In the *Power of the Covenant* series produced by the National Spiritual Assembly of Canada, we find the following comment:

" ... we must be careful to base our comprehension of it on the Teachings rather than by comparing it to other behaviour patterns we might have observed in daily life. To understand this subject we need to clear our minds of preconceived ideas or prejudices, and approach the Teachings with the authority of the Manifestation and His Holy Text clearly before us." 5

How Do We Treat a Covenant-Breaker?

No aspect of the Bahá'í Teachings is more strongly emphasised than the imperative necessity to avoid contact with Covenant-breakers.

Examine the words used by 'Abdu'l-Bahá in this passage from His Will and Testament:

" ... one of the greatest and most fundamental principles of the Cause of God is to shun and avoid entirely the Covenant-breakers, for they will utterly destroy the Cause of God, exterminate His law and render of no account all efforts exerted in the past." 6

'Abdu'l-Bahá went further in His Will and Testament, by warning against even associating with those who themselves are in contact with a known Covenant-breaker:

"A thousand times shun his company. Take heed and be on your guard. Watch and examine; should anyone, openly or privily, have the least connection with him, cast him out from your midst, for he will surely cause disruption and mischief." 7

If one was in exceptional circumstances where contact was unavoidable, individual Bahá'ís would receive clear and protective guidance from the institutions of the Faith.

The Heart of Our Faith Is Faith in Bahá'u'lláh and in His Teachings

When we examine how we each came to become Bahá'ís, our thoughts turn to matters of belief and faith.

The following excerpt is from a letter written on behalf of Shoghi Effendi:

"The primary reason for anyone becoming a Bahá'í must of course be because he has come to believe the doctrines, the teachings and the Order of Bahá'u'lláh are the correct thing for this stage in the world's evolution." 8

If our faith in Bahá'u'lláh is to be complete, we must necessarily accept everything contained within His Revelation, even things which we may initially find quite difficult to understand. We are called to make a total commitment. As the Guardian has stated,

"Are we to doubt that the ways of God are not necessarily the ways of man? Is not faith but another word for implicit obedience, whole-hearted allegiance, uncompromising adherence to that which we believe is the revealed and express will of God, however perplexing it might first appear, however at variance with the shadowy views, the impotent doctrines, the crude theories, the idle imaginings, the fashionable conceptions of a transient and troublous age? If we are to falter or hesitate, if our love for Him should fail to direct us and keep us within His path, if we desert Divine and emphatic principles, what hope can we any more cherish for healing the ills and sicknesses of this world?" 9

"Allegiance to the faith cannot be partial and half-hearted. Either we should accept the Cause without any qualification whatever, or cease calling ourselves Bahá'ís." 10

In a similar vein, the Universal House of Justice has written:

"The Bahá'í community is an association of individuals who have voluntarily come together, on recognizing Bahá'u'lláh's claim to be the Manifestation

of God for this age, to establish certain patterns of personal and social behaviour and to build the institutions that are to promote these patterns. There are numerous individuals who share the ideals of the Faith and draw inspiration from its Teachings, while disagreeing with certain of its features, but those who actually enter the Bahá'í community have accepted, by their own free will, to follow the Teachings in their entirety, understanding that, if doubts and disagreements arise in the process of translating the teachings into practise, the final arbiter is, by the explicit authority of the Revealed Text, the Universal House of Justice." 11

Recognition and Obedience

Choosing to become a Bahá'í, accepting Bahá'u'lláh's claims to be a Manifestation of God involves a big commitment.

If we are to be true or faithful to this commitment, we have an obligation to try and live our lives according to the laws and principles He has brought. This is not always easy; however, acceptance of the Faith and obedience to its provisions go hand in hand, neither being acceptable without the other.

The range of laws, ordinances and exhortations within the teachings is very broad, from fundamental laws such as the prohibitions on alcohol and adultery and the necessity of parental consent before marriage, to those which are more subtle such as the requirement for truthfulness and the obligation to recite one of the daily obligatory prayers and read the Writings morning and evening. Although none of us is a perfect Bahá'í (since none of us can claim to be perfectly obedient to all the teachings), still God expects us to keep trying to improve ourselves.

Breaking Bahá'í Law

Just as there are a range of laws within the Faith, there are a range of ways in which the breaking of such laws are dealt with.

For instance, failure to observe laws such as those of obligatory prayer, fasting, the obligation to teach the Faith, etc, attracts no attention from the Bahá'í Administration, as they are purely personal laws having to do with the relationship between a believer and Bahá'u'lláh. In other words, when someone fails to observe such laws, it only has an effect on his or her own spiritual development.

By contrast, breaking laws such as those relating to immoral relationships, consumption of alcohol, participation in calumny or persistent backbiting will certainly attract the attention of the Administrative institutions because of the negative effects that this behaviour has on the good name of the Faith, as well as on the morale and spiritual health of the Bahá'í community. Generally speaking, when dealing with matters like this, the Institutions begin with patient and compassionate guidance, education and support, as well as admonitions and warnings, a process which often results in a change in the behaviour of the person or persons concerned. If, however, the behaviour continues in spite of this process, the matter may be referred to the National Spiritual Assembly for consideration of removal of that person's voting rights: an administrative sanction which the Guardian indicated *"is a grave matter, and involves heavy penalties spiritually."* 12

How Covenant-Breaking Differs from Breaking Bahá'í Law

Unlike breaking Bahá'í law, Covenant-breaking involves opposition to or rejection of Bahá'u'lláh or the Central Institution of the Faith, which today is the Universal House of Justice, on the part of someone who has accepted Bahá'u'lláh as a Manifestation of God, ie, a Bahá'í.

The Universal House of Justice defines Covenant-breaking as follows:

"When a person declares his acceptance of Bahá'u'lláh as a Manifestation of God he becomes a party to the Covenant and accepts the totality of His Revelation. If he then turns around and attacks Bahá'u'lláh or the Central Institution of the Faith he violates the Covenant. If this happens every effort is made to help that person to see the illogicality and error of his actions, but if he persists he must, in accordance with the instructions of Bahá'u'lláh Himself, be shunned as a Covenant-breaker." 13

It can be manifested in a great variety of ways: from declarations of prophethood (which go against Bahá'u'lláh's clear statement in the *Kitáb-i-Aqdás* that there will be no further Messengers for at least 1000 years), to rejection of elements of the Administrative Order (which was defined by 'Abdu'l-Bahá in His Will and Testament), to attempts to seek leadership within the Bahá'í community, to refusal to dissociate from known Covenant-breakers in spite of warnings to do so.

Why Is Covenant-Breaking Such a Critical Issue?

All of the above activities have one thing in common – they threaten the unity of the Faith which is its most essential characteristic.

The Universal House of Justice writes that:

> "The seriousness of Covenant-breaking is that it strikes at the very centre and foundation of the unity of mankind. If God were to allow the instruments to be divided and impaired, how then would His purpose be achieved?" 14

Without unity, the means to establishing the oneness of mankind and a New World Order would be lost. Viewed in this light, our protection of the Covenant and our defence of the integrity of our Faith is not for our own benefit, but rather for the benefit of all humanity. 'Abdu'l-Bahá asserts:

> "It is indubitably clear, that the pivot of the oneness of mankind is nothing else but the power of the Covenant ... . The power of the Covenant is as the heat of the sun which quickeneth and promoteth the development of all created things on earth. The light of the Covenant, in like manner, is the educator of the minds, the spirits, the hearts and souls of men." 15

The Role of Obedience in Maintaining Unity

Having accepted that Bahá'u'lláh is God's appointed Messenger for this day, we should have no difficulty in seeing that following the laws and commands contained in His Teachings will be the best thing not only for us personally, but also for society as a whole.

That is why, when Bahá'u'lláh refers to His Book of Laws, He says:

> "Think not that We have revealed unto you a mere code of laws. Nay, rather, We have unsealed the choice Wine with the fingers of might and power." 16

To those who are in search of certitude, the following words of Bahá'u'lláh offer tremendous reassurance:

> "O Son of Being! With the hands of power I made thee and with the fingers

6 • UNDERSTANDING COVENANT BREAKING

of strength I created thee; and within thee have I placed the essence of My light. Be thou content with it and seek naught else, for My work is perfect and My command is binding. Question it not, nor have a doubt thereof." 17

However, other passages provide a sober warning to those who, having accepted His claim to prophethood then begin to question His Revelation:

"To seek evidence, when the Proof hath been established is but an unseemly act, and to be busied with the pursuit of knowledge when the Object of all learning hath been attained is truly blameworthy." 18

The purpose of questioning, and independently investigating truth, is firstly to demonstrate that you are acting on your own behalf, and not blindly imitating others, and secondly to establish that there is only one truth, one reality, which is indivisible. There is clearly a great difference between questioning to arrive at the truth or heart of a matter, and questioning the truth itself.

Having arrived at the truth, our continuing progress along the spiritual path is to be found in following the guidance provided by God's Messenger. One of the most important ways we can express this is by supporting and being completely obedient to the Spiritual Assemblies, those Institutions which Bahá'u'lláh Himself has established to be the vehicle for the Spirit of His Faith.

The importance of this principle of obedience is that:

" ... the unity which the Bahá'í Faith is progressively establishing in the world is a unity through obedience to Divine Teachings: all other forms of unity are temporary, doomed to collapse." 19 [National Spiritual Assembly of Canada]

How does backbiting about the Local or National Spiritual Assembly, or criticising and showing disrespect towards the Universal House of Justice relate to Covenant-breaking?

Bahá'u'lláh warns the individual against backbiting in any form, because it *"quencheth the light of the heart and extinguisheth the life of the soul."* 20 How much more grave this threat, when the purpose of the backbiting is to attack the Faith itself, and destroy its life-giving unity. When individuals seek to undermine the authority of the Institutions ordained by Bahá'u'lláh Himself, it is as if they were attacking the heart of the Faith. These Institutions came into being through the operation of the Covenant established by Bahá'u'lláh. To attack these Institutions is to attack His Covenant. Shoghi Effendi affirmed that:

"To be a Bahá'í is to accept the Cause in its entirety. To take exception to one basic principle is to deny the authority and sovereignty of Bahá'u'lláh,

and therefore is to deny the Cause. The administration is the social order of Bahá'u'lláh. Without it all the principles of the Cause will remain abortive. To take exception to this, therefore, is to take exception to the fabric that Bahá'u'lláh has prescribed, it is to disobey His law." 21

Have Bahá'ís ever attacked the Administrative Order?

In a letter addressed to an individual in 1996, the Universal House of Justice had cause to address a situation developing in one country, where certain individuals had over many years *"been publicly and privily assailing the institutions of the Cause and generalising specific accusations of injustice to such an extent as to accuse the entire system of corruption, not only in practice but also in form and theory."* 22

In this same letter, the Universal House of Justice described this activity as

"... an attack on the basis of the Covenant which, alone, is the ultimate guarantee that the Faith will remain true to its divine origin throughout the centuries." 22

and went on to write: *"The point at issue has thus become that of whether believers should be permitted to continue indefinitely to undermine the faith of their fellow Bahá'ís, stir up agitation within the community, and publicly assail the theory as well as the practice of Bahá'u'lláh's Administrative Order."* 22

Given the tone of this letter from the Universal House of Justice, it is logical to assume that should a believer persist in attacking the institutions of the Faith and seek to create divisions within the community, at some point such actions may well come to be considered as the actions of a Covenant-breaker. Naturally, such a decision could be made only by the central authority of the Faith, the Universal House of Justice.

This does not mean that expressing critical thought is forbidden. Shoghi Effendi referred to the need for *"open and constructive criticism"* 23 in the conduct of community affairs, and the Universal House of Justice itself states:

"How can there be the candour called for in consultation if there is no critical thought? How is the individual to exercise his responsibilities to the Cause if he is not allowed the freedom to express his views?" 24

However, Bahá'u'lláh has rigidly excluded from His Order those destructive elements *"which must sooner or later corrupt the machinery of all man-made and essentially defective political institutions,"* 25 and in order to safeguard the community from the ruinous effects of excessive criticism, Shoghi Effendi and

'Abdu'l-Bahá before Him, provided the guidance necessary to maintain a spirit of unity in the conduct of community affairs.

The following excerpt from a letter written on behalf of Shoghi Effendi is one example of this:

> *"But again it should be stressed that all criticisms and discussions of a negative character which may result in undermining the authority of the Assembly as a body should be strictly avoided. For otherwise the order of the Cause itself will be endangered, and confusion and discord will reign in the Community"* 26

An examination of past religious history reveals that when disunity manifested itself within a particular community, the end result was the creation of a division, the formation of a further sect, or a new church. That line of action is not available to us as Bahá'ís. The Covenant of Bahá'u'lláh precludes it. We are obliged to work for unity, not to create disunity. The establishment of a new model of community life depends on it.

So What Constitutes Negative Criticism?

Negative criticism can be defined as that criticism which:

- stirs up conflict and contention
- undermines the authority of the elected Institutions
- is divisive, not aimed at the preservation of unity and the good of the Cause
- is not offered in a spirit of love for the Institutions.

Unlike present-day political systems which have incorporated criticism and conflict into their processes, the Bahá'í system was designed to allow the expression of our spiritual natures. As 'Abdu'l-Bahá states,

> *"... true consultation is spiritual conference in the attitude and atmosphere of love. Members must love each other in the spirit of fellowship in order that good results may be forthcoming. Love and fellowship are the foundation."* 27

And Shoghi Effendi writes:

> *" ... love of God, and consequently of men, is the essential foundation of every religion, our own included. A greater degree of love will produce a greater unity, because it enables people to bear with each other, to be patient and forgiving."* 28

Where there is love, the *"clash of differing opinions"* produces *"the shining spark of truth,"* 29 but where there is ego and self-interest, 'Abdu'l-Bahá describes a totally different outcome:

> *"Oh ye friends of God! Beware! Beware of differences! By differences the Temple of God is razed to its very foundation, and by the blowing of the winds of disagreement the Blessed Tree is prevented from producing any fruit. By the intense cold of the diversity of opinions the rose-garden of Unity is withered, and the fire of the love of God is extinguished."* 30

Liberty and Moderation

According to the Bahá'í Writings, everything is subject to the principle of moderation.

Bahá'u'lláh states categorically that *"whatsoever passeth beyond the limits of moderation will cease to exert a beneficial influence,"* 31 and warned that even civilisation if carried to excess would *"bring great evil upon men,"* and that its *"flame will devour the cities."* 32

While freedom of thought, freedom of expression and freedom of action are all recognised as being important ingredients to the healthy functioning of society, they still need to be tempered by moderation. Otherwise, Bahá'u'lláh declared,

> *"Liberty causeth man to overstep the bounds of propriety, and to infringe on the dignity of his station."* 33

> *"True liberty,"* He states, *"consisteth in man's submission unto My commandments..."* 33

This view may not conform with current theories about freedom; however, as Bahá'u'lláh observed,

> *"... man can never hope to attain unto the knowledge of the All-Glorious, can never quaff from the stream of divine knowledge and wisdom, can never enter the abode of immortality, nor partake of the cup of divine nearness and favour, unless and until he ceases to regard the words and deeds of mortal men as a standard for the true understanding and recognition of God and His Prophets."* 34

How then, are the limits of freedom determined within the Bahá'í community? Those limits become evident when the Bahá'ís live their lives according to Bahá'u'lláh's teachings and observe the principles underlying the correct operation of His Administrative Order. In a letter to the Bahá'ís of the United States, the Universal House of Justice observed:

> '... we come to appreciate that the Administrative Order He has conceived embodies the operating principles which are necessary to the maintenance of that moderation which will ensure the "true liberty" of humankind.' 35

Balance

Learning the Bahá'í system of Administration and especially the supreme art of consultation calls individuals to a level of maturity not possible in other systems of administration or man-made political systems. It calls for maturity, and it calls for balance.

Shoghi Effendi in a letter written on his behalf commented as follows:

> "One might liken Bahá'u'lláh's teachings to a sphere; there are points poles apart, and in between the thoughts and doctrines that unite them. We believe in balance in all things; we believe in moderation in all things ... we must not be too emotional, nor cut and dried and lacking in feeling, we must not be so liberal as to cease to preserve the character and unity of our Bahá'í system, nor fanatical and dogmatic ... " 36

In a spiritual sense, our safety is to be found in obedience to the Institutions of His Faith, and ultimately, in obedience to the body authorised to protect His Covenant today, the Universal House of Justice, described by Bahá'u'lláh as *"the source of all good and freed from error."* 37

Believers who are unsure about any issues connected with Covenant-breaking should certainly seek the assistance of their Local Spiritual Assembly, their Auxiliary Board member or assistants, or experienced believers in their community to help clarify their understanding; however, we should all have confidence in the guidance which the Universal House of Justice provides for us, obey it joyfully and wholeheartedly, renew our study of the Teachings and, for the sake of Bahá'u'lláh, strengthen our love for one another. That is how we can demonstrate the transforming power of unity, and that is what the Covenant is about.

It is not enough in this day to just have a spirit of unity. Rather, that unity must be demonstrated through the efficient and vigorous operation of the Administrative Order. The Administrative Order is the only vehicle which will enable that spirit of unity to express itself and grow to gradually embrace the whole of humanity. As Shoghi Effendi asserted:

"The Bahá'í peace program is, indeed, not only one way of attaining that goal. It is not even relatively the best. It is, in the last resort, the sole effective instrument for the establishment of the reign of peace in this world. This attitude does not involve any total repudiation of other solutions offered by various philanthropists. It merely shows their inadequacy compared to the Divine Plan for the unification of the world. We cannot escape the truth that nothing mundane can in the last resort be enduring, unless supported and sustained through the power of God." [38]

SUMMARY

Covenant-breaking is a spiritual sickness which affects the soul. It is unique to this Revelation because no past religion has had a Covenant like that established by Bahá'u'lláh.

The Covenant is that spiritual power which enabled this divine Revelation to remain intact as it moved through the various stages of its development into a world religion capable of transforming humanity into a unified global society.

Covenant-breaking is the term used to describe the activities of those few persons who, once having been followers, have turned against the Faith, **deliberately acting in a way that has threatened the unity of the community.**

It can be manifested in a variety of ways: from declarations of prophethood (which go against Bahá'u'lláh's clear statement in the Kitáb-i-Aqdas there will be no further Messengers for at least 1000 years), to rejection of elements of the Administrative Order (which was defined by 'Abdu'l-Bahá in His Will and Testament), to attempts to seek leadership within the Bahá'í community, to refusal to dissociate from known Covenant-breakers in spite of warnings to do so.

Just as some physical diseases are contagious, in like manner, **Covenant-breaking is a contagious spiritual sickness.** By merely associating with a Covenant-breaker, a person can become infected with the spirit of Covenant-breaking.

In the interest of preserving the unity of the Faith, 'Abdu'l-Bahá directs us to **shun and avoid Covenant-breakers entirely,** otherwise, He warns, they will utterly destroy the Cause of God.

Without unity, the means of establishing the oneness of mankind and a New World Order would be lost. Therefore, **protecting the Covenant and defending the integrity of our Faith is not for our own benefit, but rather for the benefit of all humanity.**

Concluding Meditation from the Writings of Bahá'u'lláh

Thou hast asked Me concerning the nature of the soul. Know, verily, that the soul is a sign of God, a heavenly gem whose reality the most learned of men hath failed to grasp, and whose mystery no mind, however acute, can ever hope to unravel. It is the first among all created things to declare the excellence of its Creator, the first to recognize His glory, to cleave to His truth, and to bow down in adoration before Him. If it be faithful to God, it will reflect His light, and will, eventually, return unto Him. If it fail, however, in its allegiance to its Creator, it will become a victim to self and passion, and will, in the end, sink in their depths.

Whoso hath, in this Day, refused to allow the doubts and fancies of men to turn him away from Him Who is the Eternal Truth, and hath not suffered the tumult provoked by the ecclesiastical and secular authorities to deter him from recognizing His Message, such a man will be regarded by God, the Lord of all men, as one of His mighty signs, and will be numbered among them whose names have been inscribed by the Pen of the Most High in His Book. Blessed is he that hath recognized the true stature of such a soul, that hath acknowledged its station, and discovered its virtues.

Gleanings from the Writings of Bahá'u'lláh, pp158-159

Entrance to courtyard at Mazraʻih

Affirmations

1. I am on a spiritual journey. I was created by God, and my soul yearns to return to God. I have fulfilled my first obligation, of recognising Baha'u'llah, (God's Messenger for this day) and acquiring the spirit of faith.

2. Now I must act. As I strive to act according to the laws and principles He has revealed, my soul will be transformed.

3. As I turn my heart to God, the lights of knowledge and certitude will envelop my soul, and God will confer a new life upon it. I will be endowed with a new eye, a new ear, a new heart and a new mind.

4. I am responsible for my own spiritual development and transformation. As I study the Writings, my appreciation of the greatness of this Revelation grows and my desire to share this knowledge with others grows.

5. As I develop my spiritual qualities, it becomes easier for me to subdue my ego. Self-sacrifice means overcoming the lower side of my nature and strengthening my spiritual nature.

6. I cultivate a sense of spirituality by praying, reading the Writings and meditating on the Word of God every day. This keeps me spiritually alive and strong in my faith, even through difficult times.

7. I am firm in the Covenant when I am forgetful of self, and when I act in faith, relying only upon the assistance of God. My greatest desire is to surrender my own will to the will of God.

8. I have a powerful vision in my mind of how this Faith will transform society and ultimately create a new civilisation. My continuing study of the writings of Shoghi Effendi is giving depth and perspective to that vision.

9. Acknowledging the flow of divine authority from Baha'u'llah, through 'Abdu'l-Bahá, and then to the Guardian and the Universal House of Justice is the foundation of my firmness in the Covenant. I demonstrate this firmness in my attitude towards, and obedience to, the Institutions of His Faith.

10. I consciously try at all times to help create a loving, spiritual atmosphere within my community. It is the spirit of sacrifice which maintains and strengthens the spirit of unity. I acknowledge that sometimes I may need to sacrifice my personality to some extent in order that the spirit of unity be strengthened.

11. I am part of a spiritualising process which will lead eventually to the establishment of a spiritual civilisation. I assist this process by teaching the Faith, supporting the plans of the Universal House of Justice, and supporting the Institutions of Baha'u'llah's Administrative Order, which are the vehicles of the spirit of His Faith.

12. I am happy every day, and I know that this happiness comes with the love of God. Everything I do, I do in a spirit of service, because I want my work to be an act of worship to my Creator, and my life a preparation for the life to come.

About the Photographs

Mazra'ih - place of liberation

While imprisoned in the bleak stone fortress of 'Akká, Bahá'u'lláh longed for the beauty of the countryside. One day he remarked: *"I have not gazed on verdure for nine years. The country is the world of the soul, the city is the world of bodies."*

When He finally left 'Akká, he moved to a beautiful house named Mazra'ih, about 4 miles north of the prison city. His departure in the early days of June 1877 signalled the end of his confinement.

Bahjí

With growing numbers of visitors and pilgrims seeking Him out, in 1879 Bahá'u'lláh moved from Mazra'ih to a much larger mansion at Bahjí, also quite close to 'Akká. This place, first rented, and later purchased by the Holy family, was the scene of the final chapter of Bahá'u'lláh's earthly existence. Here He lived in utmost simplicity, surrounded by family, disciples and pilgrims until His Ascension on 29 May 1892. Today, beautiful gardens designed by the beloved Guardian circle the Mansion and the Shrine of Bahá'u'lláh - the Most Holy Spot for the Bahá'ís of the world.

Shrine of the Báb

The Báb's mausoleum was built on the spot designated by Bahá'u'lláh in 1891. 'Abdu'l-Bahá supervised its construction during one of the most difficult periods of His life. When it was completed, the precious remains of the Báb were brought from Iran amidst tremendous danger and great secrecy and finally laid to rest there by the hands of the Master Himself in 1909. The Guardian later erected the superstructure featuring the beautiful golden dome, and designed the gardens which now make it a place of great beauty - the Spot around which the Concourse on high circle in adoration.

The Shrine of the Greatest Holy Leaf, Bahíyyih Khánum

Crowning this last resting-place of the daughter of Bahá'u'lláh is a befitting monument raised by Shoghi Effendi to the one he described as *"..the outstanding heroine of the Bahá'í Dispensation"* - a woman who remained single in order to devote her life to serving her Father. Her service continued throughout the entire ministry of her beloved brother 'Abdu'l-Bahá, until finally, she was the Guardian's strongest support in bearing the enormous weight of the Guardianship after the passing of the Master. Truly the foremost woman of this Dispensation.

Sea Wall - 'Akká

'Akká, the penal colony to which Bahá'u'lláh and His family were banished in 1868. They were delivered by boat to the sea gate and forced to endure the threats and curses of a waiting crowd before being led away, and yet Bahá'u'lláh wrote of His arrival there, in a Tablet penned years before the event, stating: *'Upon Our arrival, We were welcomed with banners of light, whereupon the Voice of the Spirit cried out saying: "Soon will all that dwell on earth be enlisted under these banners."'*

Universal House of Justice

Set in gardens, high on the slopes of Mount Carmel, sits the seat of the Universal House of Justice, housing the council chamber of the Supreme Body of the Bahá'í Faith. This beautiful building with its classical column, is clad in marble chosen to resist the weathering of a thousand years.

REFERENCES

Chapter 1 'THE HEART'
1. Bahá'u'lláh, *Gleanings*, p65
2. Bahá'u'lláh, *Arabic Hidden Words*, No.59
3. Bahá'u'lláh, *Tablets of Bahá'u'lláh*, p221
4. Bahá'u'lláh, *Gleanings*, p278
5. Bahá'u'lláh, *The Seven Valleys and The Four Valleys*, p35
6. 'Abdu'l-Bahá, *Bahá'í World Faith*, p262-263
7. Bahá'u'lláh, *Gleanings*, p126
8. Bahá'u'lláh, *Gleanings*, p156
9. 'Abdu'l-Bahá, *Paris Talks*, p66
10. Bahá'u'lláh, *Arabic Hidden Words*, No. 3
11. Bahá'u'lláh, *Arabic Hidden Words*, No.4
12. Bahá'u'lláh, *Arabic Hidden Words*, No.11
13. Bahá'u'lláh, *Arabic Hidden Words*, No.12
14. Bahá'u'lláh, *Arabic Hidden Words*, No.19
15. Quoted by Bahá'u'lláh, *Kitáb-i-Iqán*, p101
16. Bahá'u'lláh, *Gleanings*, p160
17. Bahá'u'lláh, *Arabic Hidden Words*, No.20
18. The Báb, *Selections from the Writings of the Báb*, p157
19. Bahá'u'lláh, *The Seven Valleys and the Four Valleys*, p6
20. Bahá'u'lláh, *The Seven Valleys and the Four Valleys*, p7
21. 'Abdu'l-Bahá, *The Promulgation of Universal Peace*, p296
22. Bahá'u'lláh, *Arabic Hidden Words*, No.40
23. Bahá'u'lláh, *Arabic Hidden Words*, No.15
24. Bahá'u'lláh, *Gleanings*, p292
25. 'Abdu'l-Bahá, *Some Answered Questions*, p208
26. 'Abdu'l-Bahá, *Some Answered Questions*, p144
27. 'Abdu'l-Bahá, *The Promulgation of Universal Peace*, p188
28. Bahá'u'lláh, *Kitáb-i-Iqán*, p236
29. A.Taherzadeh, *The Covenant of Bahá'u'lláh*, p262
30. Bahá'u'lláh, *Kitáb-i-Aqdas*, p19
31. 'Abdu'l-Bahá, *Some Answered Questions*, p276
32. Bahá'u'lláh, *Gleanings*, pp288-289
33. Bahá'u'lláh, *Tablets of Bahá'u'lláh*, p268
34. Bahá'u'lláh, *Kitáb-i-Iqán*, p8-9
35. 'Abdu'l-Bahá, *Bahá'í World Faith*, p363
36. Shoghi Effendi, from a letter written on his behalf to an individual dated 11 April 1949, quoted in *The Compilation of Compilations, Vol 1*, p229
37. Shoghi Effendi, from a letter dated 30 May 1949, quoted in *Light of Divine Guidance, Vol.2*, p86
38. Bahá'u'lláh, *Persian Hidden Words*, No.31
39. Bahá'u'lláh, *Persian Hidden Words*, No.48
40. Bahá'u'lláh, *Persian Hidden Words*, No.76
41. Bahá'u'lláh, *Persian Hidden Words*, No.52
42. Bahá'u'lláh, *Arabic Hidden Words*, No.13
43. Bahá'u'lláh, *Arabic Hidden Words*, No.10
44. Bahá'u'lláh, *Arabic Hidden Words*, No.5
45. Bahá'u'lláh, *Persian Hidden Words*, No.3
46. Bahá'u'lláh, *Persian Hidden Words*, No.32
47. Bahá'u'lláh, *Epistle to the Son of the Wolf*, p25
48. Bahá'u'lláh, *Gleanings*, p185
49. Bahá'u'lláh, *Kitáb-i-Iqán*, pp195-196

Chapter 2 'UNDERSTANDING AND VISION'
1. Bahá'u'lláh, *Gleanings*, p193
2. Bahá'u'lláh, *Tablets of Bahá'u'lláh*, p35
3. Bahá'u'lláh, *Kitáb-i-Iqán*, p198
4. Bahá'u'lláh, *Kitáb-i-Iqán*, p199-200
5. Bahá'u'lláh, *Kitáb-i-Aqdas*, p73
6. Shoghi Effendi, *God Passes By*, p110
7. Bahá'u'lláh, *Kitáb-i-Iqán*, p172
8. Shoghi Effendi, *The World Order of Bahá'u'lláh*, p148
9. Rúhíyyih Khánum, *The Priceless Pearl*, p375
10. Bahá'u'lláh, *Gleanings*, p99
11. Shoghi Effendi, *The World Order of Bahá'u'lláh*, p19
12. Shoghi Effendi, *The World Order of Bahá'u'lláh*, p19
13. Shoghi Effendi, *The World Order of Bahá'u'lláh*, p43
14. Shoghi Effendi, *The World Order of Bahá'u'lláh*, p163
15. Shoghi Effendi, *The World Order of Bahá'u'lláh*, pp 42-43
16. Shoghi Effendi, *The World Order of Bahá'u'lláh*, pp 203-204
17. Shoghi Effendi, *Messages to the Bahá'í World*, p155
18. Shoghi Effendi, *The World Order of Bahá'u'lláh*, p170
19. Shoghi Effendi, *The World Order of Bahá'u'lláh*, p170
20. The Universal House of Justice, *Wellspring of Guidance*, p133
21. Shoghi Effendi, *The Promised Day is Come*, p1
22. Shoghi Effendi, *The Promised Day is Come*, p2
23. The Universal House of Justice, *Wellspring of Guidance*, pp133-p134
24. Shoghi Effendi, *The World Order of Bahá'u'lláh*, p170
25. Rúhíyyih Khánum, *The Priceless Pearl*, p384
26. Shoghi Effendi, *The World Order of Bahá'u'lláh*, p170
27. Shoghi Effendi, *Messages to the Bahá'í World [1950-1957]*, p123
28. Shoghi Effendi, from a letter written to an individual believer dated 5 April 1942, quoted in *The Compilation of Compilations*, Vol 1, p381

REFERENCES

29. Shoghi Effendi, *The World Order of Bahá'u'lláh*, p46
30. Shoghi Effendi, from a letter to an individual quoted in *The Compilation of Compilations*, Vol ll, p197.
31. Horace Holley, preface to 1955 edition of *The World Order of Bahá'u'lláh*, xii
32. 'Abdu'l-Bahá, *The Promulgation of Universal Peace*, p60
33. Shoghi Effendi, *Directives from the Guardian*, p86
34. Shoghi Effendi, from a letter written on his behalf to an individual, published in *Lights of Guidance*, p134 (originally published in *Bahá'í News* No.58, January 1932, p1)
35. Shoghi Effendi, *Citadel of Faith*, p149
36. Shoghi Effendi, *Citadel of Faith*, p125
37. Bahá'u'lláh, quoted by Shoghi Effendi in *The World Order of Bahá'u'lláh*, p186
38. Bahá'u'lláh, *Tablets of Bahá'u'lláh*, p125
39. Shoghi Effendi, *The Promised Day is Come*, p15
40. Shoghi Effendi, *The World Order of Bahá'u'lláh*, p187
41. Bahá'u'lláh, *Tablets of Bahá'u'lláh*, p171

Chapter 3 'COVENANT'

1. 'Abdu'l-Bahá, *Selections from the Writings of 'Abdu'l-Bahá*, p228
2. 'Abdu'l Bahá, *Selections from the Writings of 'Abdu'l-Bahá*, pp208-209
3. H.M.Balyuzi, in his book *Bahá'u'lláh*, pp117
4. H.M.Balyuzi, in his book *Bahá'u'lláh*, p117-118
5. Bahá'u'lláh, *Gleanings*, p70
6. H.M.Balyuzi, in his book *Bahá'u'lláh*, p118
7. 'Abdu'l-Bahá, *Bahá'í World Faith*, p425
8. 'Abdu'l-Bahá, *Star of the West*, Vol. 3, no.14, p9
9. A.Taherzadeh, in his book *The Revelation of Bahá'u'lláh*, Part 2, pp287-288
10. 'Abdu'l-Bahá, *Bahá'í World Faith*, p425
11. The Universal House of Justice, from a letter to an individual, 23 March 1995
12. Shoghi Effendi, *The World Order of Bahá'u'lláh*, pp21-22
13. *The Power of the Covenant, Part 1*, p3 (National Spiritual Assembly of Canada)
14. 'Abdu'l-Bahá, *Bahá'í World Faith*, pp357-358
15. 'Abdu'l-Bahá, *Bahá'í World Faith*, p248
16. 'Abdu'l-Bahá, Tablet, quoted in *Star of the West, Vol.8*, p218
17. 'Abdu'l-Bahá, *Tablets of 'Abdu'l-Bahá, Vol. 1*, p83
18. 'Abdu'l-Bahá, *Paris Talks*, p110
19. Shoghi Effendi, from a letter written on his behalf to an individual believer, 19 November 1945 quoted in *Lights of Guidance*, p542
20. Quoted by A.Q. Faizi in the Epilogue to *Stories from the Delight of Hearts*, p162

21. 'Abdu'l-Bahá, *Paris Talks*, p80
22. 'Abdu'l-Bahá, *Bahá'í World Faith*, p383
23. Shoghi Effendi, *God Passes By*, pp216-217
24. Shoghi Effendi, *God Passes By*, p281
25. Bahá'u'lláh, *Gleanings*, p253
26. Bahá'u'lláh, *Gleanings*, p79
27. Bahá'u'lláh, *Gleanings*, p212
28. Bahá'u'lláh, *Gleanings*, p285
29. Bahá'u'lláh, quoted in *The World Order of Bahá'u'lláh*, p186
30. Bahá'u'lláh, quoted in *The World Order of Bahá'u'lláh*, p40

Chapter 4 'THE ADMINISTRATIVE ORDER'

1. Shoghi Effendi, *God Passes By*, p18
2. Shoghi Effendi, *God Passes By*, p324
3. Shoghi Effendi, *The World Order of Bahá'u'lláh*, p195
4. Shoghi Effendi, from a letter written on his behalf, 16 June 1945, quoted in *Lights of Guidance*, p1
5. Shoghi Effendi, *The World Order of Bahá'u'lláh*, p19
6. *'The Power of the Covenant' Part 1*, p11 (National Spiritual Assembly of Canada)
7. Bahá'u'lláh, *Kitáb-i-Iqán*, pp155-156
8. Shoghi Effendi, *Letters from the Guardian to Australia and New Zealand 1923-1957*, pp80-81
9. The Báb, *Selections from the Writings of the Báb*, p161
10. Shoghi Effendi, from a letter written on his behalf, quoted in *Arohanui: Letters to New Zealand*, p33
11. Bahá'u'lláh, *Arabic Hidden Words*, No.2
12. Bahá'u'lláh, *Tablets of Bahá'u'lláh*, p27
13. 'Abdu'l-Bahá, *Some Answered Questions*, p309
14. Bahá'u'lláh, *Tablets of Bahá'u'lláh*, p67
15. Bahá'u'lláh, *The World Order of Bahá'u'lláh*, p203
16. Universal House of Justice, *Wellspring of Guidance*, p131
17. Shoghi Effendi, *The World Order of Bahá'u'lláh*, p43
18. 'Abdu'l-Bahá, *Secret of Divine Civilization*, p66
19. Shoghi Effendi, *The World Order of Bahá'u'lláh*, p195
20. Shoghi Effendi, *Light of Divine Guidance*, Vol.1, p182
21. A.Taherzadeh, *The Covenant of Bahá'u'lláh*, p266
22. Shoghi Effendi, published in *The Compilation of Compilations*, Vol.II, p42
23. 'Abdu'l-Bahá, *Some Answered Questions*, p158
24. Bahá'u'lláh, *Tablets of Bahá'u'lláh*, p156
25. Bahá'u'lláh, *Gleanings*, p177

REFERENCES

26. *The Power of the Covenant, Part 1*, p14 (National Spiritual Assembly of Canada)
27. Shoghi Effendi, from a letter written on his behalf to an individual, dated 11 April 1949, published in *The Compilation of Compilations*, Vol l, p229
28. Bahá'u'lláh, *Kitáb-i-Aqdas*, p21
29. Shoghi Effendi, *Light of Divine Guidance*, Vol.2, p89
30. Shoghi Effendi, from a letter written on his behalf to an individual, 1 Nov 1950, published in *The Compilation of Compilations*, Vol.ll, p135
31. Shoghi Effendi, *Unfolding Destiny*, p7
32. 'Abdu'l-Bahá, *The Promulgation of Universal Peace*, p72
33. Marzieh Gail, "Primer for Bahá'i Assemblies," *World Order Magazine*, Vol X, No.7, October 1944
34. Shoghi Effendi, *The World Order of Bahá'u'lláh*, pp9-10
35. Shoghi Effendi, from a letter written on his behalf to an individual believer, 25 April 1945, published in *The Compilation of Compilations*, Vol.II, p14
36. Shoghi Effendi, from a letter written on his behalf to an individual believer, 14 Oct 1941, published in *Lights of Guidance*, p79
37. Shoghi Effendi, in a letter written on his behalf to the National Spiritual Assembly of the United States & Canada, dated 10 Dec 1933, quoted in *The Compilation of Compilations*, Vol.II, p133
38. Shoghi Effendi, from a letter written on his behalf to an individual believer, dated 4 Oct 1950, published in *Lights of Guidance*, p404
39. A.Taherzadeh, *Trustees of the Merciful*, p54
40. Shoghi Effendi, from a letter written on his behalf to an individual believer, dated 17 Oct 1944, published in *Unfolding Destiny*, p440
41. From a letter written on behalf of Shoghi Effendi to the Bahá'i youth attending Green Acre Summer School, 4 August 1946, 19 Sept 1946, quoted in *Lights of Guidance*, p638
42. Shoghi Effendi, *The World Order of Bahá'u'lláh*, p144

Chapter 5 'THE INDIVIDUAL AND THE COMMUNITY'

1. 'Abdu'l-Bahá, *The Promulgation of Universal Peace*, p316
2. Shoghi Effendi, *God Passes By*, p59
3. Shoghi Effendi: *Arohanui: Letters to New Zealand*, pp 74-75
4. 'Abdu'l-Bahá, *Star of the West*, Vol.5, p65, 24 June 1917 (Vol.8 , no.6)
5. Shoghi Effendi, *The Advent of Divine Justice*, p6
6. A.Taherzadeh, in his book *The Revelation of Bahá'u'lláh*, Vol. 3, p35

7. Shoghi Effendi, from a letter written on his behalf to an individual, 8 Jan 1949, published in *Unfolding Destiny*, p454
8. Shoghi Effendi, from a letter on his behalf, 31 May 1934 to two believers, quoted in *The Compilation of Compilations*, Vol II, pp133-134
9. Shoghi Effendi, *Messages to America*, p28
10. Shoghi Effendi, from a letter written on his behalf, 4 April 1947, published in *Light of Divine Guidance*, Vol2, p64
11. Shoghi Effendi, *Messages to America, 1932-1946*, p28
12. Shoghi Effendi, from a letter written on his behalf, 5 September 1946 to an individual, quoted in *The Compilation of Compilations*, Vol II, p16
13. Shoghi Effendi, from a letter written on his behalf, 26 October 1943 to an individual, published in *The Compilation of Compilations*, Vol II, p112
14. Shoghi Effendi, from a letter written on his behalf, 14 October 1941 to an individual, published in *The Compilation of Compilations*, Vol II, p59
15. Shoghi Effendi, *Dawn of a New Day*, p180
16. Bahá'u'lláh, *Gleanings*, pp 244
17. Shoghi Effendi, from a letter dated 11 April 1949, published in *Light of Divine Guidance*, Vol.2, pp83-84
18. Shoghi Effendi, from a letter, 4 April 1930, published in *Light of Divine Guidance*, Vol.1, p34
19. 'Abdu'l-Bahá, *Bahá'i World Faith*, p363
20. Shoghi Effendi, *Directives from the Guardian*, p86
21. Shoghi Effendi, *Bahá'i Administration*, p72
22. Bahá'u'lláh, *Persian Hidden Words*, No.56
23. Shoghi Effendi, *Directives from the Guardian*, p27
24. Bahá'u'lláh, *Gleanings*, p261
25. 'Abdu'l-Bahá, *The Divine Art of Living*, p18
26. 'Abdu'l-Bahá, *Japan Will Turn Ablaze*, p11
27. 'Abdu'l-Bahá, *The Divine Art of Living*, p15
28. 'Abdu'l-Bahá, *Selections from the Writings of 'Abdu'l-Bahá*, p127
29. Shoghi Effendi, *Directives from the Guardian*, pp86-87

Chapter 6 'UNDERSTANDING COVENANT-BREAKING'

1. 'Abdu'l-Bahá, Tablet to an individual, October 1921, published in *Lights of Guidance*, p183
2. From a letter written on behalf of the Guardian to the National Spiritual Assembly of the United States of America, 11 April 1949, published in *Lights of Guidance*, p188
3. From a letter written on behalf of the Guardian to an individual believer, 23 January 1945, published in *Lights of Guidance*, p185

REFERENCES

4. From a letter of the Universal House of Justice to the National Spiritual Assembly of the United States, 19 July 1964, published in *Lights of Guidance*, p186.
5. *The Power of the Covenant*, Part 2. p11 [National Spiritual Assembly of Canada]
6. 'Abdu'l-Bahá, *Will and Testament of 'Abdu'l-Bahá*, p20
7. 'Abdu'l-Bahá, *Will and Testament of 'Abdu'l-Bahá*, p21
8. Shoghi Effendi, from a letter written on his behalf to an individual, 5 July 1947, published in *Lights Of Guidance*, p70
9. Shoghi Effendi, *Bahá'í Administration*, pp 62-63
10. Shoghi Effendi, from a letter on his behalf to an individual, 12 June 1933, published in *Directives from the Guardian*, p11
11. The Universal House of Justice, from a letter to an individual, dated 2 July 1996
12. Shoghi Effendi, *Unfolding Destiny*, p213
13. From a letter of the Universal House of Justice to an individual, dated 23 March 1975, cited in *The Power of the Covenant*, Part 2, p7 [National Spiritual Assembly of Canada]
14. From a letter of the Universal House of Justice to an individual, dated 23 March 1975, cited in *The Power of the Covenant*, Part 2, p9 [National Spiritual Assembly of Canada]
15. 'Abdu'l-Bahá, cited in *God Passes By*, pp238-239
16. Bahá'u'lláh, *Kitáb-i-Aqdas*, p21
17. Bahá'u'lláh, *Arabic Hidden Words*, No 12
18. Bahá'u'lláh, *Kitáb-i-Iqán*, p147
19. *The Power of the Covenant*, Part 2. p36 [National Spiritual Assembly of Canada]
20. Bahá'u'lláh, *Gleanings from the Writings of Bahá'u'lláh*, p264
21. Shoghi Effendi, from a letter written on his behalf to the National Spiritual Assembly of the United States and Canada, 30 May 1930, quoted in *Lights Of Guidance*, p2
22. The Universal House of Justice, in a letter to an individual, dated 2 July 1996
23. From a letter written on behalf of Shoghi Effendi to an individual, dated 13 December 1939 published in *The Compilation of Compilations*, Vol.1, p452
24. The Universal House of Justice, in a letter to Bahá'is of the United States, 29 December 1988
25. Shoghi Effendi, *The World Order of Bahá'u'lláh*, p154
26. Shoghi Effendi, from a letter written on his behalf to an individual, 13 December 1939, published in *The Compilation of Compilations*, Vol.1, p452
27. 'Abdu'l-Bahá, *The Promulgation of Universal Peace*, pp 72-73
28. Shoghi Effendi, *Directives from the Guardian*, p75
29. 'Abdu'l-Bahá, *Selections from the Writings of 'Abdu'l-Bahá*, p87
30. 'Abdu'l-Bahá, *Tablets of 'Abdu'l-Bahá*, p431
31. Bahá'u'lláh, *Tablets of Bahá'u'lláh*, page 169
32. Bahá'u'lláh, *Gleanings from the Writings of Bahá'u'lláh*, pp341-342
33. Bahá'u'lláh, *Gleanings from the Writings of Bahá'u'lláh*, p335
34. Bahá'u'lláh, *Kitáb-i-Iqán*, pp 3-4
35. The Universal House of Justice, in a letter to Bahá'is of the United States, 29 December 1988
36. Shoghi Effendi, from a letter written on his behalf to an individual, dated 5 July 1947
37. 'Abdu'l-Bahá, *Will and Testament of 'Abdu'l-Bahá*, p14
38. Shoghi Effendi, from a letter written on his behalf to an individual, dated 25 September 1933, published in *The Compilation of Compilations*, Vol.II, p192

BIBLIOGRAPHY

'Abdu'l-Bahá

Paris Talks, Addresses given by 'Abdu'l-Bahá in Paris in 1911-1912: London: Bahá'í Publishing Trust. 11th ed. 1962.

The Promulgation of Universal Peace, Talks Delivered by 'Abdu'l-Bahá During His Visit to the United States and Canada in 1912. Compiled by Howard MacNutt: Wilmette: Bahá'í Publishing Trust 1922-1925. 2nd ed. 1982

The Secret of Divine Civilization. Translated by Marzieh Gail and Ali-Kuli Khan: Wilmette: Bahá'í Publishing Trust, 1957. 3rd ed. 1975.

Selections from the Writings of 'Abdu'l- Bahá. Compiled by the Research Department of the Universal House of Justice. Haifa: Bahá'í World Centre 1978.

Some Answered Questions. Collected and translated from the Persian by Laura Clifford Barney. Wilmette: Bahá'í Publishing Trust, 1930. 3rd ed. 1981.

Tablets of 'Abdu'l-Bahá Abbas. Vol. 2. Chicago: Bahá'í Publishing Society, 1909.

Will and Testament of 'Abdu'l- Bahá. Wilmette: Bahá'í Publishing Trust, 1944. 2nd ed. 1971.

'Abdu'l-Bahá and Shoghi Effendi

Japan Will Turn Ablaze. Tablets of 'Abdu'l-Bahá, Letters of Shoghi Effendi and Historical Notes about Japan. Tokyo: Bahá'í Publishing Trust. 1974.

The Báb

Selections from the Writings of the Báb. Compiled by the Research Department of the Universal House of Justice and translated by Habib Taherzadeh *et al.* Haifa: Bahá'í World Centre, 1976.

Bahá'u'lláh and 'Abdu'l- Bahá

Bahá'í World Faith, Selected Writings of Bahá'u'lláh and 'Abdu'l-Bahá .Wilmette: Bahá'í Publishing Trust, 1943. Rev. ed. 1956.

The Divine Art of Living, Selections from the Writings of Bahá'u'lláh and 'Abdu'l-Bahá. Compiled by Mabel Hyde Paine. Wilmette: Bahá'í Publishing Trust, 1944. 4th rev.ed. 1979.

Bahá'u'lláh

Epistle to the Son of the Wolf. Translated by Shoghi Effendi. Wilmette: Bahá'í Publishing Trust, 1941. 2nd ed. 1953.

Gleanings from the Writings of Bahá'u'lláh. Translated by Shoghi Effendi. Wilmette: Bahá'í Publishing Trust, 1939. 2nd rev. ed. 1976.

The Hidden Words of Bahá'u'lláh. Translated by Shoghi Effendi. Wilmette: Bahá'í Publishing Trust, 1939.

The Kitab-i-Iqán, The Book of Certitude, revealed by Bahá'u'lláh. Translated by Shoghi Effendi. Wilmette: Bahá'í Publishing Trust, 1931. 2nd. ed. 1950.

The Seven Valleys and the Four Valleys. Translated by Marzieh Gail. Wilmette: Bahá'í Publishing Trust, 1945. 3rd. rev. ed. 1978.

The Kitáb-i-Aqdas, the Most Holy Book of Bahá'u'lláh. Bahá'í World Centre, Haifa. 1992.

Balyuzi, H. M.

Bahá'u'lláh. Oxford: George Ronald 1963. 2nd. ed. 1974.

Faizi, A.Q.

Stories from the Delight of Hearts. The Memoirs of Hájí Mírzá Haydar-'Alí. Translated and abridged by A. Q. Faizi, Los Angeles: Kalimat Press. 1980.

Rabbani, R.

The Priceless Pearl. London: Bahá'í Publishing Trust. 1969.

BIBLIOGRAPHY

Shoghi Effendi

Arohanui, Letters from Shoghi Effendi to New Zealand. Fiji: Bahá'í Publishing Trust. 1982.

The Advent of Divine Justice. Wilmette: Bahá'í Publishing Trust. 1939 3rd. Ed. 1969.

Bahá'í Administration, Selected Messages 1922 - 1932. Wilmette: Bahá'í Publishing Trust 1928. 7th. ed. 1974.

Citadel of Faith, Messages to America, 1947 - 1957. Wilmette: Bahá'í Publishing Trust. 1970.

Dawn of a New Day, Messages to India 1923 - 1927. New Delhi: Bahá'í Publishing Trust. 1970.

Directives of the Guardian. India: Bahá'í Publishing Trust. 1973.

God Passes By. Wilmette: Bahá'í Publishing Trust. 1944. ed 1974.

Letter written on behalf of Shoghi Effendi to an individual, dated 5 July 1947

Letters from the Guardian to Australia and New Zealand, 1923 - 1957. Australia: National Spiritual Assembly of the Bahá'ís of Australia Inc. ed. 1971.

Messages to America, Selected Letters and Cablegrams Addressed to the Bahá'ís of North America, 1932 - 1946. Wilmette: Bahá'í Publishing Committee. 1947

Messages to the Bahá'í World 1950 - 1957. Wilmette: Bahá'í Publishing Trust 1951. 2nd. Ed. 1971.

The Light of Divine Guidance, The Messages from The Guardian of the Bahá'í Faith to the Bahá'ís of Germany and Austria. Hofheim-Langenhain: Bahá'í -Verlag, 1982.

The Promised Day Has Come. India: Bahá'í Publishing Trust. Reprint 1976.

The World Order of Bahá'u'lláh, Selected Letters by Shoghi Effendi. Wilmette: Bahá'í Publishing Trust 1938. 2nd revised ed. 1974.

Unfolding Destiny, Messages from the Guardian of the Bahá'í Faith to the Bahá'ís of the British Isles. United Kingdom: Bahá'í Publishing Trust. 1981.

Taherzadeh, A.

The Covenant of Bahá'u'lláh. Oxford: George Ronald. 1992.

The Revelation of Bahá'u'lláh,. Oxford. George Ronald. Vol. 2, 1977. Vol. 3, 1983.

Trustees of the Merciful. London: Bahá'í Publishing Trust. 1972.

Universal House of Justice

Wellspring of Guidance, Messages 1963 - 1968. Wilmette: Bahá'í Publishing Trust. 1976.

Letters to Individuals

Letter from the Universal House of Justice dated 23 March 1995

Compilations

Compilation of Compilations, 1963 - 1990, Prepared by the Universal House of Justice. Australia: Bahá'í Publications. 1994.

Lights of Guidance, a Bahá'í Reference File, compiled by Helen Hornby. India: Bahá'í Publishing Trust. 1983

Power of the Covenant, Parts 1 & 2. National Spiritual Assembly of the Bahá'ís of Canada. 1976.

Periodicals

Star of the West, Vols .3,5,8. Oxford: George Ronald. Reprint 1978.

World Order, Vol X. No. 7, October 1944

INDEX of SUBTITLES

Chapter 1
The Heart   11 - 21
Developing Our Spiritual Nature 11
The Journey of the Soul 13
The Object of Our Search 14
Acquiring the Spirit of Faith 14
Becoming Stronger in Your Faith 15
How Does Somebody Love God? 16
The Importance of Recognising the
Manifestation of God 17
Good Deeds Alone Are Not Enough 17
Testing Our Faith -the Beginning of Growth 18
The Heart Must Love God 19
Love Transforms, and Love Changes Our Reality 20
Summary of Chapter 1 21

Chapter 2
Understanding and Vision   22 - 37
The City of Certitude 22
What Is This City? 23
The Writings - Reading to Understand 24
Shoghi Effendi - the Importance of
Reading His Writings 25
Understanding the Revelation of Bahá'u'lláh 25
Taking the Administrative Order into Our Vision 26
A Pattern for Future Society 26
Vision of the Future - Looking Ahead to the Goal 27
Stages in the Development of the
Faith of Bahá'u'lláh 28
Two Divine Processes 28
Plans - Realising the Vision, Step by Step 30
A Great Spiritual Battle 31
The Suffering of Humanity 32
A Vision That Prepares Us to
Withstand Hidden Tests 32
Materialism - a Universal Threat 33
When the Lamp of Religion Is Obscured 34
Effects on Character 35
Summary of Chapter 2 37

Chapter 3
The Covenant and Its Place in Our Lives   38 - 49
The Covenant and the Heart 38
The Covenant and the Messengers of God 39
The Covenant and Religion 40
What Happened in Previous Religions? 40
The Covenant Today 41
Distinguishing Characteristics of the
Bahá'í Revelation 41
Relating the Covenant to the Individual 43
Keeping Our Thoughts on the Spiritual Kingdom 44
The Importance of Remaining Firm
in the Covenant 45
Covenant-Breaking 46
The World as a Patient 46
The Prescription 47
Unity- the Yardstick 47
The Nature of Covenant-Breaking 48
Summary of Chapter 3 49

Chapter 4
The Administrative Order   50 - 65
The Main Characteristic of the Formative Age 50
The Bahá'í System - Channelling the Power 50
Diving Authority Expressed as Love 51
Divine Authority Now Expressed
Through Institutions 52
The Emergence of the Principle of Justice 53
Unity and Peace - the Fruits of Justice 54
Building Divine Government -
How Challenging Is That? 55
The Principle of Obedience 56
Practising Obedience 57
The True Source of Law 58
The Flow of Divine Authority 58
Separating Principles from Personalities 59
The System Is Perfect (we are not) 60
Spiritual Conference 60
Finding the Balance Between Form and Spirit 61
The Value of a Visible Example 62
Summary of Chapter 4 64

Chapter 5
The Individual and the Community   66 - 78
Sacrifice and Sacrifice 66
The Battleground Within 67
The Power of Unity 68
Contributing to Unity - a Personal Challenge 68
Attitude Is Critical 71
We in the West 73
Being Happy 74
Summary of Chapter 5 77

Chapter 6
Understanding Covenant-Breaking   79 - 92
A Brief History 79
Are There Different Degrees of
Covenant-Breaking? 80
How Do We Treat a Covenant-Breaker? 81
The Heart of Our Faith In Bahá'u'lláh and In His
Teachings 82
Recognition and Obedience 83
Breaking Bahá'í Law 83
How Covenant-Breaking Differs from
Breaking Bahá'í Law 84
Why Is Covenant-Breaking Such a Critical Issue? 85
The Role of Obedience in Maintaining Unity 85
So What Constitutes Negative Criticism? 88
Liberty and Moderation 89
Balance 90
Summary of Chapter 6 92